Rebel Monk

Rebel Monk

Legend of Adi Shankaracharya

Hindi edition Winner of Valley of the Words Award 2021

Rajeev Sharma

Published by
PRABHAT PAPERBACKS
An imprint of Prabhat Prakashan Pvt. Ltd.
4/19 Asaf Ali Road,
New Delhi-110002 (INDIA)
e-mail: prabhatbooks@gmail.com

ISBN 978-93-5521-291-7
REBEL MONK
novel by Shri Rajeev Sharma
(English translation of VIDROHI SANNYASI)

Translated in English
Dr. Sonia Singh Kushwah

Edition
First, 2022

Price
₹ 350.00 (Rupees Three Hundred Fifty only)

Printed at
R-Tech Offset Printers, Delhi

To

Revered grandfather **Janakram**,

who strengthened intense nationalism and

the spirit of sacrifice in our lineage,

and his sister, our elder aunt Annapurna,

an Annapurna in the real sense.

Who is he?
Miraculous boy
the victorious crusader
magnetic personality
saffron monk
tireless traveller
great organiser
nation builder
law maker
exceptional orator
amazing poet
revolutionary messenger
epoch initiator
exceptional motivator
social reformer
spokesperson of the Vedas
compassionate saint
or
incarnated Lord Shankar
Shankar Embodied!

Opinions

Shri Shankar was a pioneer in the great wisdom and a great soul born in Mother India. He was a great philosopher who gave systematic form to Advaita Vedanta. A true philosopher, steadfast logical, dynamic personality and great moral spiritual force, his power of understanding and interpretation was limitless.

—Swami Sivananda

~✦~

At the young age of thirty-two, Shankar integrated sages and monks, knowledge and compassion, which reveal that India had given birth to such a sublime person.

—Will Durant

~✦~

The only man, whose companions were enlarged wisdom and deep sympathy. Measuring the length and breadth of the entire India and conquering its mind and heart is a unique event in history and even in Indian history. Shankar conquered mind and heart of the people. He founded the empire of devotional sentiments, love and spiritual idealism. From the example of Shankar, we can guess the greatness of that person, who has shown such a path to the world.

In Shankar, we find a harmonious blend of intellectualism and sentimentalism towards the common man. Today in India, if there is one historical figure who supports intellectuals and common people, he is Shankar.

—Swami Rangnathanand

~✦~

In a short life span of thirty two years, Shankar did many long-term assignments and left an indelible impression on India with his strong mind and affluent personality which is unfathomable even today. He was a rare blend of philosopher and scholar, agnostic and mystic, and poet and saint, as well as he was a practical reformer and organiser. He created ten religious orders for the first time in a Brahmanical framework, of which four are still alive. These four places have been pilgrimages of India even before, but now they have become more important.

—Jawahar Lal Nehru

~✤~

Shankara's life seems to be a combination of many paradoxes. He was a rare combination of philosopher and poet, scholar and saint, mystic and religious reformer. The effort to delineate him brings multidimensional virtuous picture of his personality. One sees him in his youth as a fearless and steadfast logician engaged in intellectual ambition, another accepts him as a master of tactful politics, who tried to instill the mantra of unity among the people, in the view of the third he is sober philosopher, trying to unequivocally explain the discrepancies of life and thought with unparalleled understanding, and for the fourth, he is the mystic who is the greatest of all. A few universal minds have been born like him.

—Dr. S. Radhakrishnan

~✤~

Westerners can hardly imagine a personality like Sri Shankaracharya. We are filled with wonder and delight to see the devotion of saint Francis of Assisi, the intellectualism of Abelard, the power and independence of Martin Luther and the political prowess of Ignatius Loyola, but who can imagine getting every virtue gathered in one person.

—Sister Nivedita

Few Questions and Answers

I was introduced to Adi Shankaracharya by venerable father Late Shri Ramnarayan Sharma. I must have been eight or nine years old, when he returned after a long journey, as usual with many books, the most interesting of them was the life story of Adi Shankaracharya, which was more captivating than any of the comics.

The legend, inscribed on my child mind forever and this novel is the manifestation of that.

This book is actually a combined effort of my innumerable well wishers, relatives and kind hearted Indians, who have helped invaluably to collect material from every corner of the country. This book is an outcome as an interest returned for the affection that I received from distant Kaladi to Kedar. From Srinagar to Kamrup-Kamakhya and from Calcutta to Kochi, the name of Adi Shankar was like a torchbearer to illuminate my path. While searching the footprints of that great traveller, it was not known when the circumambulation across India was completed effortlessly.

Most of the people of modern India are alien to his persona and work. Those who are familiar with him, have an image of a traditional religious master in the mind instead of an image of an innovator *karmayogi*, revolutionary reformer and the architect of a unified nation. His exceptional personality was worshiped the most, but understood the least. He stands on the apex of the most misunderstood great heroes of our nation in the history. He was addressed as disguised Buddha in his life time, then why to feel surprised at the ignorance of today. Have you ever thought that our present-day India is left only between the quadrilaterals of the four monasteries established by him? So did he foresee future fragmentation of this nation centuries ago?

This novel has been written for the younger generation more than our generation, which has to face the same cultural and social catastrophe, which Adi Shankar faced in his times.

Every reform becomes a stereotype over a period it is the habit of history to witness every revolution becoming hypocritical and free warriors becoming dictators. While being a monk, he had the courage to say that I am neither an idol nor a worshiper, nor am I a priest, nor religion, nor caste.

Adi Shankaracharya has the answers to all the questions of today's youth, their curiosities and frustrations as well. Who else would be the outstanding management guru than him who changed the consciousness and the ways of life of the entire nation, which he started from a village in Kerala centuries ago.

The monks who were beyond all the disciplines of the world, he organised them into arenas and *ashrams*. He made them disciplined and organised. The conflict between Buddhism and Hindus was pacified. Shaivas, Vaishnavas, Shakyas, Ganapathis–all were put together in one thread.

I hope that this story of that wonderfully brilliant child, the miraculous teenager and the charming young Shankar may light up your life and the story might unfold the mystic episodes of his life.

Independence Day, 2022

—Rajeev Sharma
Kipling Court, Pench
National Park,
Dist. Sivani, M.P.

Gratitude

Shankaracharya Swami Swaroopanandji Maharaj, Dandi Swami Sadanandji Maharaj, Brahmachari Sushilanandji, Ms. Swarnima Shukla, Ms. Nilamani Dubey, Narsinghpur, Trilok Singh Jat, Umesh Sharma, Jhoteshwar, Late Dr. Vinay Jain, Santosh Dwivedi, Journalist Saji Thomas, Arun Tripathi.

Manager Shri Shankaracharya Janmabhoomi, Ashram Kaldi, Shri Iyerji, Ramakrishna Mission, Trivandrum, Dr. Atmaram Singh, Gwalior, Ms. Shalini Jain, Parasia Shri Ganesh Kumar, Shri Iyer, Deputy Engineer, Bhopal.

My personal staff—

Private Secretary, Shri K.K. Khare, Shri Prem Narayan Sahu, Shri Manoj Pandey, Shri Liaquat Ali, Shri Deepak Dhauran, Mantralaya Bhopal, Steno Shajapur Shri Purushottam Levy, Shri Akshat Bhatnagar, Shri Varun Joshi, Handicrafts Corporation Bhopal Shri Dinesh Rajput.

To all the relatives including my better half Rajini and daughters Sanghamitra-Charumitra.

—Rajeev Sharma

Preface

From the day the idea dawned to me until it shaped into the book,the unseen has been working through me, guiding me and inspiring meto be on a life long journey with Adi Shankracharya. I began writing 'Rebel Monk' to spread the immortal message of legendary master Adi Shankaracharya among the youth of the country. This beautiful journey has been no less than a miracle as it derives me to be the best version of myself and 'Rebel Monk' is a natural result of pure grace. The garland of my words is strung together with the essence of truth. I bow to the Himalayan Master Adi Shankracharya, for making me an instrument to sing this long lyric in prose.

I am indebted and thank Dr. Sonia Singh Kushwah for translating the book in English. I am also thankful to my childhood friend Dr. Atmaram Singh Kushwah without whom this book could not have been possible.

I hope this English version will also receive the same affection from the readers as well and be a great success in unfolding the mystic life of Adi Shankaracharya for the modern mind. I am equally eager for the Bangla and Kannad editions of Rebel Monk.

Shruti smruti purananam alayam karunalyam
Namami Bhagvatpad Shankaram lok Shankaram

—Rajeev Sharma

Contents

1

Dharmarajeshwar

In the Malwa region of Central India lies Dashpur, an ancient city. It is said that Mandodari, wife of Ravana belonged to this place. The same Dashpur was witness to a rise of rivalry between the Shaivites and Vaishnavites. A huge 10-feet high and eight-faced *shivalinga* stands in the adytum of the sky-kissing *shivalaya* in Dashpur. River Shivna runs its course adjacent to the temple and in it the devotees take a holy dip and experience joy. The centre of attraction is the *shivalinga* in eight up-and-down postures – humorous, auspicious and calm, exhibiting the nine emotions. In the conflict between the Shaivites and Vaishnavites, the pagoda collapsed and the idol disappeared.

A similar kind of discord arose some 100 kms away at another place with the same faith. In the direction of Rajputana, away from Dashpur, lies an awesome temple of Shiva, named Dharmarajeshwar. This temple is a marvellous example of Shaivite sculpture. As a matter of fact, this temple is not on the ground; it is three floors under the ground as a result of which the temple courtyard is not visible from the surface. It becomes visible only when one reaches very close to the ground and gazes down. The rocks are cut into steps from the top to descend to the temple courtyard.

Brick, mortar or lime was not used to build Dharmarajeshwar; nor even stones or pieces of marble. In fact, this temple was made by creating a space in the rock in such a manner that the peaks of the roof pillar were built by carving on the same rock.

In the same Dharmarajeshwar temple, a huge fair is held

on every Shivaratri. Local faith makes people believe that if a Shivaratri night is spent in the temple, it reduces one's birth-and-death cycle and helps one to draw one step closer to receiving *moksha* (salvation).

Due to this belief, a day before Shivaratri festival, devotees walk towards the temple with their families, chanting and singing devotional songs to spend their night in Dharmarajeshwar. It is a religious fair – an occasion for thousands of people to gather and buy all kinds of paraphernalia for performing *puja* – food items, clothes, utensils and jewellery. Additional attractions at the fair are sports activities, magicians, snake-charmers and jugglers performing their tricks.

This time there is no hustle and bustle of Shivaratri. A still silence pervades Dharmarajeshwar. The veteran priest, dull and depressed, is seated on the rock in the courtyard of the temple. The enmity between the Shaivites and Vaishnavites has disrupted the spontaneous and joyous festivities of the place and the life of this entire region. The Shivaratri festival is more like an individual event rather than a collective one due to the rampant fear of bloodshed. People are furious, simmering with anger beneath the mantle of peace.

The situation is tense, but under control because both the sides are secretly engaged in preparing for their next move. The Shaivites claim the temple to be theirs because the lustrous, black *shivalinga* has been shining in it for centuries. The Vaishnavites feel a prick in their hearts as two hundred years ago, there existed an idol of Lord Padmanabha and the Shaivites had challenged their faith by establishing a *shivalinga* here, while the Vaishnavites were helplessly forced to remain silent in front of the mighty Shaivites. Now, when the Shaivites have been removed from power, the desire to eradicate the injustice done earlier to the Vaishnavites has become stronger.

The common masses are fed up with the discord between Shaivites and Vaishnavites and are engaged in hearing Gautam

Buddha's message of peace and non-violence. As obvious, in the battle of two, it is the third party which stands to benefit and this very thing has happened in Dharmarajeshwar. A grand Buddhist monastery is being constructed by labourers working day and night. It however remains unknown as to from where the Buddhist monks have arrived in a large number. Surprisingly, these monks are skilled people as city planners, water managers, craftsmen, engineers, etc. They have hollowed out the huge mountain ranges with their chisels and various tools to erect prayer halls, stone *stupas*, meditation halls, restrooms, etc. Villagers are arriving to see the vast monastery carved with intricate craftsmanship. They are awestruck at the sanctity and the prayers conducted in this beautiful Buddhist monastery.

The young monks are also the centre of attraction for all, as this new religion is appealing to everyone. As a result, silence pervades in the ancient kingdom of Dharmarajeshwar. Veteran priests are worried as the devotion and offerings in the temple have reduced to such an extent that it is difficult to offer any to the idols. On the other hand, the grain stores of the Buddhist monasteries are full to the brim.

It seems that the bells of the temple have forgotten to ring. The echo of the victorious sound of '*Buddham sharanam gacchami*' ('come under the shelter of Buddha') is gathering speed. Even the priest fears that the wave of the new religion will sweep away the egoistic existence of Shaivites and Vaishnavites. The clear flow of Sanatan Dharma has accumulated a lot of garbage. The relationship between the great principles of the *Vedas* and *Upanishads* in practical life are dwindling.

Religious freedom has given way to religious anarchy in the hands of the wicked. No one remembers as to when the merit-based *varna* system got changed into the birth-based *varna* system. As a result, the toil and sweat of the labourers have now come to be looked down upon and the dignity of the traditional craftsmen has been lost.

A sudden rise is observed in the number of unexpected and hypocritical people. Even after the existence of thirty-three crore deities, the self-proclaimed deities and idols of different gods are beginning to wither. Like termites, all kinds of ills had started creeping into the mindset of the society thus rendering it hollow.

Gone was the era of the great emperors. There was an increase in the dwarf-like successors, who devoted all their might to dominate in their small territories. Chivalry and valour was replaced by conspiracy, political diplomacy by cunning moves and good governance by shameless plunder. From Kerala to Kedarnath, misguided but amazing ideas of religious deceit, social rancour, intellectual stupidity began to develop everywhere. '*Sarve bhavantu sukhinah*' (may all remain happy) – the great message – was being crushed under the feet of selfish desire.

The sanctity of the temple was replaced by filth, abuse of mutual understanding had now replaced chanting, and devotion had given way to hypocrisy. The impersonators through their glib tongue were becoming the saviours of the society, while the austere practices of the ascetics and *yogis* had been confined to the forests. A warrior was needed to fight all these perversions and lead the wandering souls to the righteous path, to expose the hypocrisy, to engage the scholars in practical solutions and to free the scriptures from the clutches of a handful of selfish preachers and intellectuals and make them reach the general public. It was tough – tough like swimming against the flow of time, but it was necessary.

□

2

The Abode of Good Fortune

On the southern peninsula of India, among the clumps of coconut and arecanut trees, lies a unique land known as God's own country, the abode of good fortune – Kerala. The west coast of Kerala is washed by the blue waves of the Arabian Sea and while the east is adorned with a mountain range covered with lush evergreen trees.

The word 'Kerala' is derived from *kera*, meaning 'coconut' and *alaya*, which means 'home'. It is no wonder that there are rows of coconut trees everywhere – coconut trees in front of the house and coconut trees even in the backyard. It is said that in ancient times, it was the kingdom of the demon-king, the great Bali. Frightened by his valour, the gods requested Lord Vishnu to free them from the misdemeanours of this mighty demon-king. Lord Vishnu incarnated as Vamana and asked Bali, known as the great donor, for a donation of three feet of earth. Bali readily agreed. As soon as he said 'yes', Vamana measured the entire earth in three steps. Committed to his words, the great Bali did not back down from his word and left for the Himalayas, donating the entire earth to the Brahmins. Since then, once a year, he is said to come to Kerala for four days to meet his devotees and these four days are celebrated as the festive days of Onam festival.

Another legend devotes the origin of Kerala to Lord Parshuram who wanted a beautiful, lush green place for the Brahmins to live in. At the request of God Varuna, he threw his axe from the top of the mountain to the south coast of India. The sea humbly moved away from the path of his axe and as a result, the Malabar caost came into existence, spreading from Kanyakumari to Gokarna.

Parshuram settled the Namboodiripad Brahmins on this Malabar coast. Namboodiri is actually Namapudri or Nampuri. In Malayalam, *namya* means 'faith' and *puri* means 'the people with complete belief in Brahmin scriptures'. The same Nampuriya is Namapoodiri Brahmin.

Spread from Tavancore to Cochin, the Nampuri Brahmins are considered venerable, reverend and highly noble. They adhere religiously to the rules laid by Lord Parshuram and are respected in society for their physical and religious purity and moral conduct. They do not lack wealth as they own the best pieces of land. On the land of Malabar, they are revered like living gods. Nair, Pulayar, Bedar, Paria, Ilwah, Shanar – all are conscious of their honour and dignity.

In each village, their dwellings are in an *agrahari,* i.e. the front area is developed on the best plots, where the Brahmins dwell as teachers and priests as well as temple servants, gardeners and musicians, etc.

The cool breeze that arises from the coconut, banana, betel nut and mango trees in the foreground of Kaladi village, situated on the banks of River Purna, gives divine delight. Regardless of the hot sun, the birds sit on the branches, in the cool shade of mango trees to communicate with each other. The banana trees are in full bloom. Bunches of bananas hang like chandeliers amidst which a large red flower attracts butterflies.

Today is the fifth day, the *panchami* of the month of *Vaishakh* and the shrill cries of a newborn echo in the majestic residence of Shivguru and Vashishta, the most eminent couple of the iconic *agrahara* in Kaladi.

The baby born today is the fruit of this couple's pleasure and penance. The joyous mother, forgetful of the delivery pains, beholds and pats the newborn baby on her bed. On seeing joy and satisfaction on her face, one is tempted to envy her. There is a sense of gratification on her beautiful face as her neighbours are ready to extend their service and cooperation in these happy moments.

Shivguru, her husband, is amazed at the unique experience of becoming a father of one who has made him happy. He is thankful to God, pleased like a joyous winner. Sometimes he goes out to check on his servants who are distributing sweets to their neighbours and acquaintances and sometimes he enters the room where the women congregate and drive him away out of hesitant shyness, forcing him to depart upon hearing their hilarity.

Outside, his brothers, friends and acquaintances shower good wishes on the happy occasion of the birth of the child and soon can be heard the melody of female voices that resonate from a room. There is a celebration in the entire *agrahara* today and why not considering that everyone's good wishes are with this couple.

These moments of ecstasy and pleasure have come after a long wait in the life of this gentle couple. Shivguru is reminded of the past as the family history plays like a movie in his mind. His scholarly and respected father Pandit Vidhyadhar left him in a *gurukul* to acquire knowledge. Today is his last day in the *gurukul*. A thought has been churning in the mind of the child Shivguru since many days.Today, on the last day of the *gurukul*, he has built enough courage to present his thoughts to his *guru*; so he reaches his hut.

When he notices his *guru* absorbed in the evening prayers, he sits on the ground in the salutation posture. When *guruji*, after his evening prayer, notices his beloved disciple bow before him with respect, he says, "Long live! Shivguru, son, your education is complete; now you can return to your parents and please them."

"*Guruji*, my mind wishes to remain engrossed in your presence to learn, teach, pray and seek devotion."

"No Shivguru, your celebacy period is over. Now it's time to take charge of family; it's not proper to delay the marriage rituals. Your parents wish to marry you to continue with the dynasty tradition. Only after living in the family, you may think of renunciation."

Guru's order do not interest Shivguru and the former senses the attitude of the disciple. So he asks the reason. Bowing his head, Shivguru pleads very politely, "*Guruji*, what you say is true, but it is also said in the *Vedas* that those who are detached from the world, can straight away take to *sanyas ashram*; even celibacy. Yes, those who enjoy the world are free to adopt the institution of marriage. I have been interested in spirituality since childhood, so let me delve in devotion."

□

3

Guru-Disciple Dialogue

"Lo! Shivguru, look who's behind you?"

Obeying *guru's* command, Shivguru turns back and finds his revered father Pandit Vidyadhar standing. Awestruck, he bends down to touch his father's feet. Vidyadhar embraces the son to his heart. He gives a shawl, *srifal* and *dakshina* to *guruji* and requests permission to take Shivguru home.

Shivguru suppresses his reluctance in mind but obeys the command of his father and *guru* to return.

Vidyadhar tests the knowledge of his son, while returning home. Through *Vedas* and *Upanishads,* his discussion covers philosophy, economics, Ayurveda and miscellaneous subjects. When the father finds his son mentally enriched, his happiness multiplies fourfold. His son's education, modesty and ideal behaviour bring more laurels to his reputation.

When the fragrance of the virtues of Shivguru start spreading in the area, the proposals of a suitable girl from an elite clan start reaching them. Every day attractive proposals are received at his door. Vidyadhar and his wife approve of one among these girls of noble descent. She is very beautiful and carries the name Vishishta.

At the destined hour, with the recitation of Vedic *mantras,* the marriage between Shivguru and Vishishta is solemnised.

The life-chariot of the new couple begins to tread the canonical Vedic path. Their life becomes sweet as a flute playing the notes of mutual love and dedication. They remain immersed in the joy of performing early morning bath, worship, recitation, charity, hospitality and self-study.

Due to their noble deeds, the family's wealth, prosperity and fame accumulate doublefold every day and fourfold every night. Years pass in this manner and immersed in their joy, Shivguru and Vishishta reach a turning point at an age where the youth bids farewell and maturity of age peeps through the grey hair.

One day, Vishishita, concerned at the maturity of age visible in the grey hair and sadness of Shivguru, says, "Dear husband, there is one thing I wish to say."

"Yes, yes, say it."

"My lord, the garden of our family continues to remain empty. I have heard that Lord Shiva is Ashutosh and if we worship Lord Shankar, our emptiness can be filled."

"You are right. I am ready."

The husband and wife make the necessary arrangements and climb the Shri Vrishadari mountain to pray to Lord Shiva. Here the lively statue of Lord Chandra Mollishwar fulfils the desires of devotees. The husband and wife immersed in austerity with devotion, wish for a son. Several months pass, their penance gets tough and tougher day by day. Surviving on snacks and fruits, their fasting shrinks their body though their mind becomes greener with every creeper of faith.

One day, while meditating on their wish for a son in deep sleep, Shivguru sees Lord Shiva, with his long hair-locks, ask, "Son, why are you undergoing such tough austerity? Tell me what is in your heart?"

"God, I desire the birth of a son..."

"Son, I am pleased with your penance. Tell me, what kind of a son do you want? "

"God, grant me a long-lived omniscient son."

The Lord laughs aloud and replies, "If you wish for an omniscient son, then he will not have a long life and if you want a son with a long life, then he will not be omniscient. Tell me, what kind of a son do you want? Omniscient or one blessed with a long life?"

"God, grant me a son as glorious and omniscient as you are."

"As you wish; your wish will be fulfilled. I myself will take birth as your son. Your penance is complete; now go home".

Shivguru suddenly wakes up. He describes his dream to his wife. The husband and wife duly end their penance by performing *yajna, puja,* donations and return home happily.

Shivguru and Vishishta devote most of their time in praying to Lord Shiva. Immersed in their devotion, one day Vishishta conceives. Day by day, a new aura and glow appears on her face. She can feel divinity around her. Often she gets awakened, shocked at seeing a vision of herself riding on a white bull, in her dream. One day, in her dream, she sees that she is engaged in a debate and emerges victorious from it. At times, she sees people worshipping her. As the delivery time approaches, Shivguru devotes his time to Vishishta's diet, comfort and convenience, religiously gazing at her radiant face. One Sunday afternoon, when it is *Vaisakha Shukla panchami,* he hears the newborn's cries amid his wife's delivery pains. The newborn's cries revive Shivguru from his nostalgia to return to the present moment of blissful celebration.

Soon they find that it is time to name their son received through Lord Shiva's blessings and name him Shankar. The family priest arrives and while drawing up the newborn's horoscope, he gets pleasantly awestruck! He exclaims, "Shivguru, you are very fortunate. Your son is blessed with divinity and will incarnate."

The generous Shivguru becomes more and more humble in moments of happiness.

□

4

Mesmerising Child

The dear child of Shivguru and Vishishta becomes the apple of everyone's eyes just like the dear Lord Krishna was of Nand Baba of Gokul and Mother Yashoda. Not only the near and dear ones of the family, even the neighbours, well-wishers, friends, acquaintances and whosoever sees this little baby, gets eager to hug him. Radiant and fair complexion like a full moon and large eyes cannot be said to be less than the lotus; his long, sharp nose, beautiful lips, uplifted forehead, beautiful ears, shapely body make everyone say that the Creator had utilised all his craftsmanship to shape his body. His playful postures, pleasing disposition, attractive smile, soft touch, rhythmic body movements are the centre of attraction and affection for all. He wakes up in the mother's lap, but after listening to her voice, the neighbours leave work to play with him and after hugging him affectionately, countless streams of motherly affection spring up so much so that the mother who has given birth to the infant has to remain patient to receive him back. The infant Shankar is the centre of everyone's affection. This favourite toy-like child, for the adolescent girls of the family or whosoever visits, encourages one to hold him and shower affection upon him. The passing villagers are satisfied to catch a glimpse of him on their way and when they are unable to see him, they hope for fulfilment of their desire the next time.

The happy days fly past no time. No one pays heed to the passage of time or when the waxing moon (*Shukla paksh*) came or when the waning moon (*Krishna paksh*) went away. Everyone is fascinated by the child Shankar. His presence is like the presence of a full moon in the sky of Kaladi. He possesses Shivguru's wisdom, penance and Brahmin aura in the blood itself, along with his mother's polite simplicity, spontaneity and brighteness that glow on his face. The power of sharp wit is his. Even before the first birthday, he begins to stand and walk on his own.

When Shivguru sits down to pray, the little Shankar goes and plonks himself on his father's lap to observe the whole process with keen interest. He follows his father perform the idol for the bath, apply sandalwood paste, offer whole grain rice (*akshat),* panicum (*durva*) and flowers. When the father prostrates, the little Shankar also bows his forehead at the feet of the deities. During his worship, when Shivguru sings Vedic hymns, the child loves to listen intently and later in his own voice, repeats the words that come to his mind. In his father's company, he learns new words every day. While learning the words, he instinctively starts repeating the full *mantra*. His intelligence and memory begin to shine under the umbrella of Shivaguru's affection. Considering his child as a gift of God, Shivguru begins to impart the knowledge of *Upanishads* and the *Vedas* in the same way as his wife breastfeeds the child. The ritualistic influence of the husband and wife has such an effect on the child that by the time he is two-years old, Shankar is able to memorise the scriptures. Hearing his recitation, the beholders remark that such brilliance marks the anticipation of accumulated virtues earned in previous births, while others would say that, like Abhimanyu, he too had learned all the scriptures in his mother's womb. This conjecture is very close to the truth because whichever scripture Shivguru reads, he would often discuss it in detail with his better half and which the infant, in his mother's womb, would have heard.

□

5

Abode of Father

Malayalam and Sanskrit, both the languages are gradually drawing close to the little child's heart. While worshipping the *mantras* which Shivguru sings, the child repeats them verbatim without making any mistake. Hearing the *shloka* from him, Shivguru would call out to the wife.

Vishishta Devi would emerge from the kitchen to enter the prayer room. The happy Shivguru tells her, "He seems to have an excellent memory, Vishishta."

"How, my Lord?"

"Whatever he hears, he remembers it the same way. When I chant the *mantra*, your beloved son repeats the same," said an excited Shivguru.

"Let me hear too..."

"Son, recite for me again..."

Whatever the little child had heard, he recites again. On hearing this, the husband and wife become ecstatic.

Vishishta hugs her son to her heart, "My Shankar will bring fame to your name, Lord."

"Yes Vishishta, it will happen by the grace of God. After all, I prayed to God for a glorious son."

On recalling the dream, the husband and wife forget their bliss for a moment. An unfamiliar fear and apprehension begins to trouble their mind. They remember that their beloved son has only eight years to live. Two years have already been spent...Oh God!

Vishishta hugs her Shankar close to her heart and thinks,

'Dreams are dreams.' Days and nights are spent by Shivguru in the worship of God. The son's shrieks, naive mischiefs, eccentricities give him pleasure, but the fear of his son's short life makes his heaven a hell every moment.

Shivguru, swinging between hope and despair, regrets asking God for an extraordinary son. He tells himself, 'I wish I had asked for a son, who would have a long life, but who need not be extraordinary or be blessed with sharp intellect; then he would have stayed with us.'

The desire in human heart pricks like a thorn in the heart of a person like him, while Vishishta is lost in her son day and night. In the arena of the world, there is nothing more interesting and pleasing like the activities of an infant.

Unaware of the happiness and grief of his parents, the child, with his talent, evolves with evey passing day. Shivguru thinks that in the fifth year, after performing his *upanayana* ceremony, he would send Shankar to the *gurukul*. The wife, however, is not in favour of sending her small child as she does not want to be separated from him even for a moment. She tells herself that when the time comes, it will be seen.

Shankar has now begun to read Malayalam texts with his father and as a playful game, he gleans through the pages of most of the scriptures kept in his father's reading room. Shivguru regularly starts to teach his son. Father's affection and teaching are conducted and blended simultaneously.

At times Vishishta feels that her husband is transferring too much knowledge to the little child. So she, in humour, takes away her son to place him in her lap at which Shivguru has to wind up his reading sessions.

Uncertainty characterises human life. Apprehension at his son's short life plagues Shivguru every day. One day leaving Shankar asleep, Vishista Devi, like every other day, leaves her bed early morning and goes to make offerings to the deity after arranging things for her husband to bathe and worship.

After preparing the *prasad* (offering), she reaches the temple of her home, but is unable to find her husband anywhere. She goes towards the bathroom but her husband seems to be missing. The eerie silence in the house makes her rush towards Shivaguru's bed, though she is conscious that her husband would not be in bed for so long. Surprisinlgy, she finds him lying in bed. She calls out, "Lord, my Lord!"

She draws close to shake him with her hand, but finds that all is in vain. His body is icy cold.

Merged in the Supreme essence, Shivguru leaves Vishishta Devi and the little Shankar orphaned. Vishishta Devi clings to the body and wails. Her cries disrupt the peace of the morning. All the friends and neighbours rush to her house with dejected faces. The happy family of Vishishta is devastated. She has fallen from the paradise of contentment into a blind well of grief. Such is the strike by the thunderstorm of Fate! How can she bear this onslaught of sorrow? She can only weep, so she sobs hysterically.

There is a gathering of men outside the house. All are grief-stricken. Shivguru was a gentle, cooperative and humble man. Everybody feels sad at the loss of his life.

After wails and cries, the family and friends begin to engage in preparing for conducting the rites on his final journey. In the flames of the funeral pyre, the body of Shivguru merges into the Divine.

Kaladi today is grieved, silent and shocked.

At the loss of her husband, Vishishta hits her head, oblivious to the fact that her little child had woken up among the wails and uproars. Little Shankar tries to fathom the reason for the presence of so many people in his house. Why is his mother crying in such a grievous tone?

Seeing the young child awake, a woman compassionately picks him up, takes him and puts him in Vishishta's lap. Little Shankar looks with innocent eyes at his mother's tears and wipes them with his tiny palms.

The women utter, "Vishishta, now don't cry. The baby is scared to see you weep. Look at him and try to forget your grief. Make this young sapling flourish with a heavy heart."

Wallowing in the deep darkness of sorrow, Vishishta hugs the little Shankar close to her heart with silent tears streaming down her face. The tears of the little boy roll down on to her back, wetting her shoulder. While trying to soothe him, Vishishta wipes away her own tears.

The scene at Shivguru's funeral is heart-wrenching. When the relatives pick up the little Shankar in their lap to make him torch the fire in the pyre, the innocent child suddenly looks grave and all eyes well up with tears.

After the rituals of death are completed, the close relatives offer a few words of compassion and return to their respective homes.

Vishishta Devi, dressed in white, continues to immerse in grief and loneliness.

The cattle in Shivguru's ranch have learned to remain calm in this moment of grief. The seemingly serene Vishishta is severely shaken at her husband's sudden demise. She does not remember to feed herself. Even the family deities have become accustomed to the darkness engulfing the house.

Distressed at her loneliness, Vishishta hands over the responsibility of her home to the neighbours and moves to her maternal home with little Shankar. She is welcomed in her father's home. No one leaves a stone unturned in making her feel comfortable. Affection is showered on Shankar as well. His shaved head looks dear to everyone, but he misses his own house. He remembers his father regularly and cries for him. He finds some consolation in his mother's affectionate lap, but it is not enough.

After a few days, nostalgia overpowers Vishishta as she misses her home. In her dream she sees her cows mooing and this makes her decide to return to Kaladi with her son.

Little Shankar is overjoyed on returning home. He goes to the cows with flattened bread. The cows also recognise him and feel satisfied. They enjoy eating bread from his tiny hands.

As her home had been lying vacant for a long time, it needs to be cleaned and rearranged by Vishishta. On hearing about her arrival, acquaintances and neighbours arrive to meet her. She enquires about the welfare of her farm and land from her servants. All are pleased at her return.

Every morning and evening, Vishishta lights the lamp to illumine the deities in the temple of her home. Her grief lies deeply embedded in her heart, unseen just as water lies underneath the soil. The young Shankar is the only support of her life. Her goal is to foster him like his father. Now she has to play a double role – that of a mother and a father. Like Shivguru, she wakes him up early in the morning, guiding him with affection. This is followed with the daily prayer ritual, after which she gives him fresh cow's milk to drink. Later, the mother and son engage in spiritual readings. The incessant reading sensitises Shankar's craving for knowledge. Besides, he plays and learns to swim. However he derives pleasure only from self-study.

Vishishta is lost in her unbearable loss, though her life is an unaffected lamp that keeps burning. She has been struck by a stroke of misfortune but her culture, education and perseverance remain intact. Her modesty patiently steers her lifeboat to the safe shores in the whirlpool of the day's problems. She is praised by everybody for her virtues. Despite the blows of pleasure and pain, Shankar steps into the fifth year of his life under the shadow of his mother's affection.

Vishishta Devi performs her son's *upanayana* ritual as deemed fit. The little Shankar is now a Brahmin wearing the sacred thread. With a heavy heart, Vishishta sends him to the *gurukul* to acquire education with children of his age.

The sobbing Visishta is cursed to bear the burden of this separation in the silent home from both her *yogi*-husband as well as her son. Her consolation, however, lies in the fact that her

Shankar would return some day after completing his education.

Like a boat she hitches a hike in the ocean of the world because her boatsman has left her in the middle of the torrent.

On the other hand, as soon as Shankar reaches his *gurukul*, he becomes the centre of everyone's affection and attraction. He is far ahead of other children of his age in his lessons. All are awestruck at his miraculous memory, sharp intellect and knowledge. It seems as if he may have learned the *Vedas*, the *Upanishads*, *Aranyakas*, geography, *Arthashastra*, grammar and *Natyasastra* in his previous birth or in his mother's womb itself.

He is able to compose aesthetic poetry. His reviews and interpretations are staggering. He has entered the *gurukul* as a learner, but his intellect is akin to a teacher.

□

6
Life in the *Gurukul*

The daily routine at the *gurukul* is tough and discipline-oriented. In the dense forest surrounded by thick trees, lies a group of huts made of coconut leaves and mud. The *gurukul* is a prestigious education centre in the beautiful lap of Nature. Here children get education under the guidance of their *guruji.* The duties of the students include getting up in the wee hours, seeking blessings by touching *guruji's* feet, retiring from day-to-day chores to sit for daily lessons before going to a maximum of five houses to beg for alms and depositing the received alms at the *ashram*. This is the sequence of daily routine. The duties of students include cleaning, fetching water to drink, bringing wood from the forest, cooking food and serving cows. All have to follow the rules of the *ashram*, whether high or low and regardless of one's status. Everyone has to follow the rules of the *ashram* without any discrimination and all the disciples are equal in the eyes of *guruji.* Eating less, observing silence, doing concentrated meditation and a sense of service are the essential prerequisites for them.

The *guruji* himself toils ceaselessly. He is an inspiration for the disciples. They follow his simplicity and good conduct. Like all other days, even today, after attending to his daily routine and meditation, Shankar ventures out to the nearby township to beg for alms. At the door of the first house, he calls out, "*Bhiksham dehi*" (give me alms).

□

7

Give Me Alms

Hearing the call "*Bhiksham dehi,* mother! *Bhiksham dehi,*" a searing pain runs through the veins of a housewife. She thinks to herself, 'It is difficult to quench my hunger due to poverty; there is not even a handful of food in the house. If only I had it, I would have given it to maintain the dignity of the house and religion.'

Distraught at her thoughts, she, however, searches in every corner of the house but discovers that there is neither money, nor food. The same voice of the Brahmin again pleads at the door, "Mother, please give me alms."

'Oh God, such helplessness!' Again the unhappy mother looks around the house with worried eyes and finally finds a dry gooseberry which is four-days old. With tearful eyes, she comes to the door. A humble boy stands at the door, waiting for alms. The woman, ashamed at her poverty, with trembling hands and tearful eyes places the gooseberry on the small palm of the boy, saying, "Child, since I am deprived and distressed, I have nothing else to give you."

The young Brahmin boy respectfully takes the gooseberry in his bowl. He seems to have gauged her poverty in a glimpse and feels compassionate to the core. He replies, "Mother, you are rich despite being poor. You had nothing, yet you gave me this gooseberry in charity and this was your greatest wealth. In fact, poor is one who, despite having wealth, is unable to donate. May Mahalakshmi, the Goddess of Wealth, bless you soon."

He then prays and invokes Mahalakshmi. The euphonious

voice of the Brahmin boy is infused with compassion. How can Mahalakshmi ignore the benefactor's invocation sung in divine language? She appears in Shankar's conscience and expresses her inability to do anything due to the family's account being devoid of any virtue.

"Oh, the mother of the world! Is anything impossible for you?"

"The account of her past birth is zero. Even if I were to give her a little, it would amount to violation of the system."

"Mother, just now she donated me a gooseberry; you too may give her the same from your treasury."

Mahalakshmi smiles at the persistent attitude of the child and relents, "I grant" and disappears.

Even in the housewife's sleep, the charming face of the brightly illumined student keeps on floating. Ah! How sweet his voice was! How brightly lit his face and how beautiful he was! With these thoughts she slips into sleep. Suddenly she hears a sound like the falling of hailstorm. 'Oh God! Without rain, from where did these tiny balls of snow come?' she says, jumping out of the bed and rushing to the courtyard. She exclaims, 'Oh God, these are golden gooseberries showered from the sky! How is it possible? They seem to be made of gold. Yes, this is gold. Oh Mahalaxmi, the benevolent! Is it an illusion or is the gold a result of the melodious hymn sung in a golden voice by that boy?'

This miracle of little Shankar becomes the subject of discussion everywhere. After all it marks only the beginning – a golden beginning!

□

8

Shadow of Mother's Affection

In two years, the meritorious Shankar completes his lessons in law, mathematics, metaphysics and philosophy, etc. through the grace of his *guru*. He does not leave but learns history, *Puranas* and *Smriti* while doing specific study of Buddhist, Jain and Charvak philosophies.

As *guruji* realises that his pupil's education has been completed, he affectionately advises Shankar to leave the *gurukul* and return home. Sadness and disappointment engulfs the *gurukul* at the news of Shankar's departure. Even his classmates do not wish to be separated from him. Everyone bids him farewell with a heavy heart.

In Kaladi, a festive atmosphere prevails at the return of Shankar as a young student. Not only Shankar's childhood mates, his neighbours, relatives and others are eager to meet him on hearing about his miraculous achievements. After an absence of two years, each one is anxious to see him.

It seems like Diwali for his mother, Vishishta Devi. She draws welcome designs *(rangoli)* at the main door of the house. The servants have hung rows of mango leaves on the doors and the door-frame is decorated with sacred banana leaves – after all, the apple of everyone's eyes has come back home.

Shankar touches his mother's feet as soon as he arrives. She hugs the son to her heart and exclaims, "Hey Shankar, you have grown so strong in two years!"

"Yes mother, the students in *gurukul* have to do a lot of

manual labour and yes mother, there I learned the art of combat too. Mother, look at my strong arms; this is a result of the practice of two years."

In response, she asks, "What kind of a *gurukul* is it? We had sent you to study the scriptures and you have come back mastering the art of warfare!"

"Mother, *guruji* says that physical strength is also needed to protect the scriptures. That's why bachelors should also develop muscle power."

This intimate and sweet discourse between the mother and son turns into a collective conversation with the arrival of relatives and childhood friends. After the cordial meeting, everyone sits down to lunch. Mother has prepared the favourite dishes of Shankar, who enjoys them to the fullest, with his friends. The look of satisfaction on her son's face after taking the meal makes Vishishta Devi pleased. After the meal and the departure of friends, the mother continues to rejoice in asking about her son's experiences at the *gurukul*.

The next day, the young bachelor takes charge of many household duties of his mother in the spirit of maternal service. He would wake up in the wee hours and engage in carrying out his mother's chores. Then take a bath, pray, meditate and read. Vishishta Devi senses and finds that her son is different from other boys. He, with a happy heart, takes to looking after his mother's comfort, while she feels satisfied.

The fame of young Shankar's erudition, eloquence and reasoning begins to spread far and wide. Curious knowledge-seekers now gather at his home. His eloquence mesmerises all and his arguments render the others speechless. His proficiency in the selection of language, style, grammar and diction integrated with his knowledge, appears divine. The ever-increasing fame of the boy attracts senior scholars to his house. On acquiring deep knowledge from the mouth of a seven-year-old child, some start to call him an incarnation of Vyas, while some others would call him Patanjali; still others would feel that Lord Gautam Buddha had arrived as an incarnation blessed with immense knowledge. His miracles are discussed everywhere.

There is also a feeling of jealousy among some of his relatives. They try to belittle him by proving him to be a magician or a hypocrite. The growing fame of the child fans the fire of jealousy and hatred in their heart.

□

9

The River Changes Course

Vishishta Devi is religious-oriented and daily walks with the villagers to bathe in the Purna river. After taking her bath, before returning home, she offers prayers at the ancestral Keshava temple.

In the summer season, the sun's rays are intensely hot. Even the air is not cool. One day, the young Shankar eagerly awaits the return of his mother after completing her daily morning routine. Usually, she would return from the temple before the rays of the sun reached the doorstep. That day, however, the sun has reached the top of the door and the day has become bright but his mother has not yet returned.

The worried child begins to walk towards the river. He can feel the intensity of the sun's heat. He moves towards the river with brisk steps, thinking why his mother had got delayed. Reaching half way, he finds his mother is lying unconscious on the path. Seeing her condition, he begins to cry and runs up to her. He pats her face, gives her water to drink and takes her to a shaded place. As she recovers a little, he holds her hands and slowly escorts her back home.

He then makes his mother lie on the bed and watches her with tears streaming down his eyes. Saddened at the mother's plight, Shankar offers sweet milk to her as she appears to be weak. His mother slowly falls asleep as if wanting to take rest.

The child Shankar gets up and goes to pray in their prayer room, "Oh God! I can't bear to see my mother in such a condition.

She is your supreme devotee. Without bathing in the Purna river and without offering prayers to you, she does not take a morsel of food. The river is far from home and despite the scorching heat of the sun, she goes to the river to bathe. Oh Lord! Please bring the river near my house, so that my mother would not have to walk such a long distance."

He continuously repeats this prayer in front of the deity with full concentration. His prayer is heard by God and the weather suddenly takes a turn. As the evening approaches, it starts to drizzle, which soon turns into torrential rain as if a war has begun in the sky with the clouds beating like drums, lightning crackling and the heat of the sun replaced with cool raindrops. It pours throughout the night. The health of Shankar's mother gradually improves and she gets busy in saving the fuelwood and household items from getting wet in the rain.

Young Shankar continues to pray the entire night. The second day it rains so heavily that the Sun-god is unable to emerge and there is water everywhere.

The third day sees the entire Kaladi city immersed in water with rainfall continuing unceasingly. The Purna river, which flows outside the village, now gets flooded with rain-water, which flows down to the village in a deluge. The villagers pray for their lives and leave their homes to seek shelter in higher places.

God listens to the prayers of the villagers and on the fourth day, the deluge recedes, bringing back the people to life. The water level of the Purna river starts to subside. When the flood waters recede completely, people find that the Purna has changed its course. It now flows from the backyard of Shankar's house in a semi-circular path towards the temple of Lord Krishna.

Shankar, grateful to God, bows his head in a humble gesture. His heart's call has been heard and accepted by the compassionate God. He wants nothing more than this. He is pleased that his mother will no longer need to walk far to bathe.

Vishishta Devi is amazed at this miracle performed by her

son. Surprised she is as she has seen with her own eyes Shankar praying to God to bring the river near her house. She considers it to be the naive imagination of a child's heart, but wonders how anyone can believe that a fantasy could come true in such a manner!

Seeing the river flow in the backyard of her house, she asks Shankar, "Son, how did you do it?"

"Mother, I did not. This was done by God. All I did was to pray to God."

"No Shankar, this is not so simple. This is something divine; how did this happen?"

"Mother, while leaving the *gurukul*, Acharya had affectionately given me this *gurumantra:* 'Whatever one asks with a pure heart from God, He does not disappoint. Only, the demand should be with full mind, full soul, full faith and full intensity'. Guruji had said that we hesitate in seeking but God never hesitates to give."

His mother is far from satisfied at the son's answer, but what greater proof was needed to prove the fact?

The residents of Kaladi soon forget their hardships caused by the flood and start bathing in the river which has now begun to flow near the village. They glow with pleasure due to the convenience in getting water to drink, to bathe and irrigate their fields. Some people in the village, close to Vishishta Devi, have knowledge about the whole event. They see Shankar's divine act with appreciation, whereas those who are jealous consider it a common geographical phenomenon, which happens many times with rivers. Unaffected by both praise and condemnation, Shankar is pleased that his mother has no longer got to walk far to bathe.

□

10
Royal Invite

How is it possible that the fame of Kaladi's miraculous child would not reach the ears of Rajashekhar, the king of Kerala? Scholars used to avail of special honours in the court of King Rajashekhar. *Pandits* and sages of the country were always invited there. The king himself was a scholar, efficient in use of both weapons and scripture and very popular among his subjects.

In a small village of his kingdom, a young Brahmin boy is said to be performing divine acts. This is informed by the king's spies who describe how the rain of gold gooseberries alleviated the grief of a poor Brahmin family. Now, on receiving the news of the river diverting its course, the king is overwhelmed with the desire to meet the child.

He sends his trusted ministers with gifts and a beautifully embellished elephant. When the ministers reached Kaladi with their state troops, a stir is created in that tiny village. The villagers, bubbling with curiosity, watch the royal troops march towards the residence of Shankar. So, they too start following behind the visitors.

The minister offers the king's invitation placed on a gold-studded plate to the child Shankar with utmost respect in his service.

The child Shankar says with firm politeness, "Oh the giver of welfare! Begging is our livelihood; deer skin we wear, serve our *guru* and perform evening prayers. We have received education in the *Vedas* and the scriptures. What do we have to do with the pastures of elephants, except for our deeds? The way you have come, you may return happily." He took a moment's pause as the minister and the court looked at his enlightened face. He further added, "Instead of inviting me, it's the duty of the king to invite and take care of the livelihood of the wise men who are engaged in pursuing the path of righteousness; make them debt-free and teach everyone to practice self-righteousness."

The royal troops, including the minister, salute him and return to the capital. On hearing this, King Rajashekhar himself arrives in Kaladi. Saints in his court also accompany him to meet this child prodigy, who is amazing; whose thoughts are evidence of his fearlessness and whose conduct is praiseworthy. When the king reaches Kaladi, he is awestruck at the divine aura surrounding Shankar. He is struck by the fair-complexioned beauty of the child-ascetic, who stands out among the Brahmins reciting the scriptures while wearing the sacred thread on their shoulders and deer skin on their body.

The young Shankar greets the king in a dignified manner. In a few moments, the king is able to gauge the maturity of Shankar's wisdom, the capacity for original thought and the promise of a bright future. He is greatly influenced by his word power, rhetoric, poetic quality and innovative thoughts. While bidding farewell to him, the king presents him with thousands of gold coins as a mark of respect, but Shankar politely declines this offer.

When the king again pleads with folded hands, a detached Shankar replies, "Oh king, I am a Brahmin and a child celibate. Gold currency is of no use to me. We have already sufficient property, which is enough for me and my mother to live on."

The generous King Rajashekhar is astounded at the qualities of renunciation and sacrifice in young Shankar. He says, "Oh, great Brahmin, you seem like a child but in fact your renunciation and sacrifice prove your maturity due to your wide knowledge. But I cannot take back what I have resolved to donate. You may distribute it among the needy."

A humble Shankar gracefully requests, "Oh king, you are the king of the land but the religion of a Brahmin teaches him to donate knowledge. To donate money is the king's endeavour; you should distribute it among the worthy recipients."

The king's insistence loses in front of the child's insistence. King Rajashekhar distributes that wealth among the Brahmins. After paying obeisance to Shankar as a teacher, the king returns to his capital. His conscience is happy as he has been able to meet a wonderful person, whose talent, like a sun, is soon ordained to illumine the nation. He is able to judge this well and feels the future safe today. He pledges in his heart to remain in touch with this child-celibate as he himself is an aesthete and an accomplished writer. It is the exceptional way in which the child discourses on subjects ranging from literature, arts, culture to spirituality and to even politics that convince the king of the former's capabilities.

Since long he had been in search of a generous *guru* who, ignorant of him being a king, would provide him guidance and communicate intelligently. Today, it seems the vacuum has been filled!

When the king returns to the palace, his family come and surrounded him. They ask with similar curiosity aboiu the miraculous child of Kaladi. Today all want to know about him!

The king narrates the whole event with all the necessary details. The curiosity is far from satiated upon hearing this part; rather, it flares up further. The story-telling activity ends when the king is seen to be feeling sleepy. The king reaches his parlour and soon drops into sleep due to the fatigue of the journey. The mind of the awakened audience begins to plan on how to meet that comely child!

On the other hand, at the door of Shankar in Kaladi, stands a crowd of curious visitors. God knows from which far off places the devotees have gathered with an ardent desire to see him. It seems that Kaladi has a fair numbr of people ready to see Shankar. The philosophers of Vedanta, the investigators of spirituality, the scholars have been coming since many days; now even the people who are suffering from worldly ailments begin to come to him with the hope of finding a cure for their malady. Poor people in want of money, rich people in thirst for more money and people in the hope of forgiveness for suffering, surround him from morning to evening. He meets all, listens patiently and treats each one's ailment. Half of the people's suffering disappears at his generous and emotional behaviour; the rest are destined to bear the fruit of their actions.

□

11

Astrologers Arrive

Even today, there is a huge line of devotees waiting since the morning. He is alleviating the pain and grief of the miserable ones and some seers, who can foresee the future, are present at his house. Vishishta Devi and Shankar treat the guests in a befitting manner. After the reception, Shankar turns to attend to the other devotees. The seers express their desire to study Shankar's horoscope. Mother Vishishta Devi with due respectful hands over the horoscope of her son.

She than asks the astrologers engaged in doing some calculations, "Oh learned Brahmins, what calculations have you been doing so religiously? Please tell me my son's future."

In response to her question, one of them remarks, "Oh respected lady, your son is very glorious because there is an incidence of descent in his birth. He will be a great transcendent, a supreme mystic."

With a doubtful mind, Vishishta Devi asks, "You tell me about his life line; how long is it?"

The astrologers reply, "Oh lady, God has ascribed a short life for your son. There is a possibility of his death at his eighteenth, sixteenth and thirty-second years of age."

Hearing this, Vishishta Devi begins to weep as Shankar is her only child and the sole support of her life. On seeing sorrow on the face of Shankar's mother, the astrologers say, "The possibility of death in your son's eighth year can be avoided by undergoing penance, but death in the sixteenth year is dependent entirely on God's compassion."

At the fear of losing her only son, tears begin to flow down the eyes of Vishishta Devi. The astrologer-Brahmins try to console her but her tears refuse to stop.

After the departure of the Brahmins, Shankar, on hearing of the predictions, decides to undergo penance. He is in his ninth year and his death is drawing near. The fire of renunciation burns in his heart and it refuses to be quenched despite his mother trying to extinguish it. Every day he seeks permission from his mother to allow him to do penance, but the mother refuses repeatedly. He finds himself caught in a dilemma between his desire and his mother's disapproval.

□

12

Purna Episode

River Purna is the lifeline as well as the centre of joy and celebration for the people of Kaladi village. Both men and women take their bath in the river in the wee hours. Children swim fish-like in the waters of the Purna. There is plenty of activity along the banks of Purna during festivals. Even a small boat race competition is organised on the river. It seems the sun emerges out of the river and the day dives to set in it. Women do not know from which place the water enters the river to strike their musical chords, nor does anyone know from where the tiny, colourful butterflies come to swarm near the banks of the river.

Even today, in the wee hours, Vishishta Devi wakes up and finds young Shankar already up and about, waiting for his mother to get up. Soon the mother and son go to bathe in the river. Arriving at the bank and descending down to the *ghat*, Vishishta pats her son's head and warns, "Shankar, don't go in deep water."

"Why mother?" the child asks with astonishment in his big eyes.

"Son, a crocodile caught a cow's calf swimming there in the evening. The villagers are claiming that a crocodile has been seen in the river."

"Okay, mother, I'll be cautious."

Descending into the river, the mother and son with folded hands bow to the holy River Purna, after which the mother goes to the women's bathing *ghat* and Shankar reaches the *ghat* meant for children. Shankar's friends are already present in the water. A daily competition to take a dip, hold one's breath and stay in the water for a long time is underway. The children are pleased to see Shankar, "Come, come...now the winner has come!"

A child is splashing water with both hands, another lies on his stomach in the river. Shankar also joins in the water-sports of the congregation with a happy heart. Mother comes out after a bath. All of a sudden, while Shankar is swimming with his friends, a turmoil occurs. People run out of the water on hearing the screams of the bewildered children. Shankar is seen screaming, "Mother! Mother! Save me. A crocodile has caught me." The other children also start shouting. In order to save her son, the worried mother jumps into the river along with other people who are bathing in the river but are unable to rescue Shankar. Caught in the clutches of the crocodile, Shankar is seen flapping his hands and feet, but the crocodile has started to drag him into deep water. A frantic Shankar appeals to his mother, "Mother, this crocodile is taking me away. Perhaps my time has come. You did not grant me the permission to do penance; without penance, there can be no salvation. If you still permit me to take the vow of abstinence, I shall inform God about my renunciation. This will bring me salvation."

Seeing no hope of Shankar escaping from the jaws of the crocodile, the mother relents, "So be it, son. I permit you to become a monk."

On getting permission from his mother, Shankar begins to pray to the deity in his mind that he accepts the life of a monk. His eyes begin to close. By now, the fishermen of the village have surrounded the crocodile. Alarmed at seeing them with sticks and net traps, the crocodile leaves Shankar and dives into the water to escape. The villagers carry the mother and son to their house. The mother is unconscious while the injured Shankar is soaked in blood. The village doctor cleans up the wounds and applies a paste of herbs to stop the bleeding. Shankar tells his mother, "Mother, I have renunciated the world to become a monk. It is forbidden for a monk to stay in the house. Henceforth, I will live under a tree."

"What is this? What you are saying, son? You are still a child. How will you survive away from home? How many days I have to live? After I die, you can leave the house. Stay with me as long as I am alive. You have some duty towards me."

Shankar replies, "Mother, it was at your approval that I took the spontaneous decision. Now if I withdraw, your words would be held to be untrue. I will have to leave the house. "

"Son," pleads Vishishta Devi, drawing a long breath, "who will feed and look after me without you? How will I live? Who will serve me and who will torch me when I die?" Saying this, Vishishta Devi begins to cry.

"Mother, don't be sad. The one who saved me from the jaws of the crocodile, the same God will protect you and me. All your needs will be fulfilled by Him. Remember, last time I had promised that I will be present to serve you as a divine vision. Mother, be patient and happily bless me, so that my renunciation and birth are meaningful."

Vishishta Devi remembers the story behind Shankar's birth. Realising that Shankar would not go back on his words and accepting it as God's will, she says, "Okay son, all my blessings are with you. May your desire be fulfilled." Saying this, she hugs the son to her heart and begins to sob. The pain at her beloved son leaving their home pierces her heart, making tears of helplessness flow from her eyes. Shankar wipes his mother's tears with his hands and says, "Mother, prepare for my renunciation as prescribed in the traditional manner in the scriptures. Arrange for a *kamandal* (water-pot), *kashay* (ochre-coloured robe) and *kopin* (loin cloth), for I will have to wear them now. Mother, I want you to dress me as a monk with your own hands."

"Alright son, the Creator had not ordained in my destiny that I should see you become a groom. I will dress you now as a monk." Saying this, Vishishta Devi resolutely wipes away her tears, washes her hands with cold water, bows her head in front of God and gets engaged in making the preparations. All the articles are collected by her before dropping off to sleep at night.

After performing her morning prayer-rituals, the mother, with tears in her eyes, offers her loving son the *kamandal, kopin* and *kashay* cloth to behold him as a monk. The villagers too are surprised to see the tender and delicate Shankar in his new garb. They begin to discuss the day's events in their own way. From the east, the Sun-god appears on the horizon, riding his chariot of seven horses. But under the sky of Kaladi is seen the shadow of a little monk stepping towards the temple of the family deity.

Sitting in the temple, in front of the family deity, he bows with emotional reverence. Thunderstorms of memories rack his brain. After offering his prayers, he stands up and comes out. The priest makes him aware of the dilapidated condition of the temple. Shankar recalls the dream in which the family deity has wished to be removed from this temple because the temple is getting decrepit due to the ravages of river water. With the consent of the villagers who follow behind him, he picks up the statue of the family deity from the sanctum of the temple and places it at a high spot. He requests the village residents to build the temple at this new spot. When he bows to take leave from his mother and the villagers, they all begin to weep, but the young monk consoles them and departs.

Today the scene at Kaladi resembles that of Ayodhya when Lord Rama must have left for 14 years of exile.

□

13

Search for *Guru*

The young renunciator from Kaladi now has to be duly initiated into a monastic life for which has to find his *guru*. All that he knows is that his journey, which started from Kaladi is slated to end in a cave where Govindapadacharya has been meditating for ages on some unknown bank of the sacred River Narmada.

But what is the route to Narmada? No one knows in Kaladi. No matter whoever he asks, he is told that it is in the north direction. 'If you go to Benaras, you will definitely reach Narmada before the dense forests of Benaras.'

The young Shankar moves towards the north, when suddenly he remembers that in his *gurukul*, as a child, when reciting the epic of Maharishi Patanjali, *guruji* had become awestruck at the tone, rhythm and melody of his voice. He hd said to the boy, "Shankar, when you shall recite the epic of Maharishi Patanjali, you shall be able to see him if you want."

Child Shankar had asked with glee, "*Guruji*, how is this possible? Maharishi Patanjali is an ancient sage, who was born ages ago. How can I see him now?"

Guruji had replied, "Dear child, it's your good fortune that Maharishi Patanjali has reincarnated and is meditating in a cave since many years. In this life, he is popularly known as Govindapadacharya. He is a great *yogi*, teacher and philosopher who is well versed in monistic Vedanta philosophy."

Guruji had affectionately continued, "Shankar, though you are my disciple, I have taught you everything as much as I knew but my knowledge is limited. I want you to achieve perfection by becoming a disciple of Govindapadacharya, who is a disciple of Guru Gaudpadacharya."

That very day, the little Shankar accepted Govindapadacharya as his future *guru*. In a dream just a few days before the renunciation, he sees his family deity, Lord Krishna asking him to leave Kaladi and go to the banks of River Narmada to become a disciple of Govindapadacharya. So he moves towards north in search of him.

On his way to the north, whosoever meets Shankar is surprised to behold him. An eight-year old, tender, innocent-looking boy with his shaved head, ochre robes, a wooden water-pot in his hand, wearing wooden sandals, a mark on the forehead and a godly sharp glint in his eyes, has set out on an endless journey on foot. Whoever sees this wonderful, comely and gentle child on the path, is shocked at such a display of celibacy for the first time. The women who see him silently utter in their hearts, 'Oh Rama, how can any parent be so ruthless as to allow his young child to become an ascetic when it is an age for him to play?'

Shankar's serene face attracts innate affection and admiration from passersby, but unaffected by it, Shankar continues to meditate on the principles of goodness. Early in the morning, during the dark hours, after attending to his daily routine, he starts his journey on foot. When the sun is bright in the afternoon, he consumes whatever he gets at a temple or a village before marching forward. It is fine if he is able to reach a village in the evening; if not or else in the midst of a dense forest, he eats some wild fruits or even if these are not available, he eats the leaves of whatever edible vegetation he finds and goes to sleep.

He comes across villagers, peasants, merchants, traders, thieves, bandits, wild animals, predatory hunters, saints, monks, detectives, foreign travellers, elusive thugs on his way, but he is so determined and undeterred that he has compassion for both the scary wild spiders and the alluring butterflies. He is so serene that even the ferocious animals that come near him become calm. His journey during the moonlit nights is enticing and easy and even the fortnight period between the full moon and the new moon does not disturb him.

His feet are no longer soft. He is least bothered by the blisters on the soles of his feet, even when some of them burst due to friction caused against the stones and pebbles lying on his path. His mind is concentrated and attracted towards an unknown and unfamiliar *guru*.

Karwar and Pandarpur are crossed and now he reaches Vidharba. His march is towards Mahakaushal in search of the great *guru* meditating on the banks of River Narmada.

He finds relief from the scorching heat of the sun when he reaches the shadows cast by the tall *sal* and teak trees in the dense forests of Mahakaushal. Heedless of the wild beasts, herds of wild elephants, monstrous forest buffaloes, terrifying pythons, venomous snakes, cunning cheetahs, predatory tigers, Shankar walks ahead with his mind focused on his goal.

The forest-gods seem to be enchanted at the fearless Shankar when they remember seeing skilled hunters falling prey in this ghostly and uninhabited forest. Here this eight-year old child keeps moving forward, uninterrupted either by Nature or by the wild beasts who keep out of his way as if they have taken the vow of non-violence.

Perceiving the mountains, valleys, rivers, villages, cities with an equal vision, he moves towards his goal. As soon as he reaches Gokarna, his classmate Vishnu Sharma joins him. It's always better to be two rather than one. The loneliness of the journey gets erased in the company of Vishnu Sharma. It becomes easier now for the two child-ascetics to travel day and night, seeking the path of River Narmada. They reach the dense forest of Mahakaushal, crossing rivers like Kaveri, Krishna, Godavari, Banganga and countless other streams. They are only aware of the enormous sea of humans they have crossed in the last few months and observed different languages spoken, different types of people engaged in different practices, celebrating different festivals, faith and creed, running countless types of business, under the rule of various kings and rulers. All they are conscious of is the sandy soil of these superficial divisions, the intimacy, the hospitality, the affection, the harmony and human compassion which are almost the same everywhere.

As they cross the coast of Travancore and Malabar, they observe the difference in language, food and hymns. The teachings of their *gurukul* become significant and useful on this journey to Jambudweep. In the *gurukul*, they had interacted with students who spoke Kannada, Malayalam, Telugu or Tamil, so they are familiar with some words spoken in these languages, while some other tasks are accomplished by gesturing and using the language of signs.

The journey becomes easy due to their knowledge of Sanskrit language. When they face any difficulty, they speak in Sanskrit and it works everywhere. On the way, they rest and beg for alms in the same spirit of reverence as observed in the monasteries of faiths like Shaivism, Vaishnavism, Buddhism Jainism, Pashupati, Shakta, etc. Shankar discovers that everyone's prayers, eulogies and texts are in Sanskrit. Even the important ceremonies, like marriage, conception, initiation, cremation are performed only in Sanskrit language. Even the illiterate masses do not seem to be dumb as they are able to comprehend Sanskrit.

From a land of betel nuts, bananas and coconuts, he feels a sense of unity and belonging in all the places and finds these three food items essential and accessible for worship all over the land.

Shankar walks day and night in search of the banks of River Narmada in order to reach his future *guru*, Govindapada. When he had left Kaladi, it was the onset of summer which is long over now. Even the four months of monsoon rain could not halt his journey. Now the winter is about to set in.

□

14

Crematorium Hunter

As the child-ascetics have not yet reached a place when they can break their journey, they continue to walk fast so as to cover as much distance as possible. That is why they have not even stopped in the previous village as they want to halt at the next village, but which is nowhere in sight. While moving ahead on their path, they notice a light in the far distance. They move stealthily towards it. The light grows bigger in size as they draw nearer to it, but when they reach it, they find that it is not a light, but flames emanating from a funeral pyre. Completely exhausted and dying of hunger, their body cries out for rest. But how can they find food in the crematorium?

Instead of going to the crematorium, they fill their stomach with water from a natural stream flowing nearby and thank God for providing it as their dinner for the night. In the far distance, a few lamps seem to flicker, but the ascetics are so tired that they presume these lights to be of some other crematorium.

They decide to spend the night on a clear rock lying on the banks of the stream, but life is not so easy. A devilish man, eager to sacrifice these youthful children, emerges from the crematorium, giggling loudly. His long, dry hair, tangled beard and moustache, a black mark on his forehead and red eyes are enough to frighten one in the eerie silence of the crematorium.

With a drawn sword in his hand, he moves forward towards the boys like an agile hunter, but the undaunted Shankar stands transfixed on his rock. Vishnu Sharma is also shocked at this macabre scene in front and thinks of picking up a big stone in self-defence. The hunter comes rushing from the front with his entire focus on the boys. Little does he know that there is a deep pit in front and falls into it wth a sword held aloft in his hand. All that there remains are his painful groans tearing in the stark silence.

While sitting on the rock, Shankar is engrossed in wondering why despite being part of the divine, man can become more beastly than any beast! The purpose of religion is to elevate man, but bigotry, confusion and superstition turn him into such a beast that even human slaughter becomes a religious duty. There is no limit to the foolishness of man.

The murderer himself gets sacrificed in the pit created to make a human sacrifice in his violent method of worship. Cautious of the incident, the child-celibates continue on their journey through the forest. Shankar notices that all is not bad or annoying in the journey. He sees the beauty of Palash forests in spring and relishes how Nature changes colour in every season. Both the child-celibates continue to walk under the sky since the time they had left home, except for the time spent in countryside villages and cities on the way. They spend most of their time in the lap of Nature, drinking the cool and pure waters of rivers and enjoying the charming company of different and attractive wild animals and chirping birds. During their journey, they also find tigers, leopards, wolves, but no one seemed as violent as a human running with the sword in that dreadful night.

The brave Shankar continues to walk with his companion, pausing only to enquire about the route on their way to River Narmada. Strangely enough, not even once have they gone astray. In the village where they stay, they are welcomed with open arms by the villagers on discovering that they are on their way to River Narmada.

The young son of the householder in whose house they have to spend the night is very religious by temperament and has already undertaken the Narmada *darshan* and a dip in the

Narmada. When Shankar asks him the route to Narmada, he becomes very happy and offers to take them there. On second thought, he remembers that number three (because there would now be three members undertaking the trip to Narmada) is not auspicious and ropes in his friend for the trip. The next morning, when the journey begins, they are now four of them walking towards the Nramada. Gradually the cold increases. The villagers have gifted them blankets which are tied on their back. They move forward, braving the cold.

These new young friends of Shankar ae somewhat shaken on learning about the distance yet left to cover. Shankar is impressed at the practical knowledge of these rural youth, who belong to the families of farmers possessed with amazing knowledge not only of crops or seeds, but also of seasons and stars.

Soon they cross a hill and descend down the slope. They notice from amidst a clump of *sal* and teak trees, a wide river flowing below. One of the young boys exclaims, "Swamiji, this is Mother Narmada."

Shankar and his young friend Vishnu Sharma are overwhelmed with reverence on seeing the sacred river. They all rush towards the river just as a calf runs to it mother-cow.

Narmada, an ancient river, nay, the most ancient river is renowned for ascetics and saints observing austerity and penance on its banks and that is why it is also known as Reva: *'Reva tire tapa: kuryat'* (on the banks of Reva, do penance). The *Vishnu Purana,* begins by echoing thus in memory of Shankar: 'In Kanarval Ganga, in Kurukshetra, Saraswati is a virtue-giver, but Narmada is a universal virtue-giver.'

One day *guruji* had taught his pupils in his *gurukul* that "purity is attained by taking a holy dip for seven days in the Yamuna, three days in the Saraswati, and by taking a holy dip for one day in the Ganga, while it is virtuous to merely behold the Narmada." On seeing the serene flow of the Narmada, eyes become moist. After taking a holy dip in it with reverence and drinking the water of the

Narmada, one's thirst gets quenched deep down to the inner self.

On seeing a festival on the banks of Narmada, the young celibates discover that it is *Makar Sankranti* on that day. A fair is organised here as people from distant lands come to take a holy dip in the Narmada on this day. After paying homage to the Narmada, everyone took a bath in its holy waters. The tribals in the area happily feed these young celibates with freshly prepared food, which is delicious, but the taste is something new. Eating wheat flour balls baked on fire and hot lentils and brinjal stuffing is a new experience for Shankar.

After the meal, they decide to take rest in the shade. As the afternoon heat reduces, they start moving in search of their *guru* while the tribals return to their homes. The music of the jungle now echoes with the melody of the twilight hour.

Shankar walks along the banks of the Narmada, while the Sun-god wishes to set. Shankar looks around and his eyes notice a shrine with the flag aflutter in the far distance. He and his companions increase their speed to reach the shrine before it gets dark. On walking some distance, they espouse fields, barns and huts of the villagers. On the way, they encounter cows returning from the forest with their cowherds. Along with them, Shankar and his companions reach the temple, where a middle-aged priest greets them and offers fresh water and delicious food. The priest even prepares beds for them to rest, but, where is rest for Shankar, who is desperate to meet his *guru*? On noticing his dedication, the priest affectionately says, "You are a bright child. You have firm determination. I have not met your *guru*, but I have heard about him from devotees who come to the Narmada. You will definitely find many saints and ascetics on the Narmada coast and you will certainly succeed."

Hearing this, Shankar's mind becomes somewhat calm. He does not even realise as to when his tired body reaches the realm of sleep.

Next day, the child-monk leaves his bed before dawn. Four

full-moon periods have passed since he had departed from Kaladi. He undertook the journey for visiting River Narmada from far-off Kerala without worrying about either day or night. He climbs down the temple platform to go and take a bath in the Narmada waters to rejuvenate. He offers his prayers on returning to the temple. Here the priest urges him to take lunch and gives him a warm farewell.

Shankar picks up his stick and vessel to proceed in search of Guru Govindapada, when he notices a cave on the banks of the Narmada, crowded with many aacetics at the entrance. He most humbly asks about Guru Govindapada after bowing humbly to the senior ascetics.

Impressed by the enlightened disposition of the child-ascetic, they all are amazed to know that this child hasd come alone from far-off Kerala to visit Guru Govindapada. Unbelievable, but true! They are thrilled. They greet the child-monk, but Shankar is anxious to satisfy his own curiosity.

□

15

Seeking Circumambulatory Guru

Shankar's fervent curiosity is satiated to hear that in this cave, Guru Govindapada has been in *samadhi* since time immemorial. Many generations of devotees have spent their life in the hope of seeing him on awakening from meditation. These ascetics have since childhood nurtured a wish for the completion of Govindapada's meditation but have aged with this desire.

A relieved Shankar questions the veteran ascetic, "Swamiji, can I behold him?"

"Yes... your devotion for the *guru* makes you eligible for it, but there is intense darkness in the cave; only with this lamp will you be able to reach him."

Shankar enters the cave excitedly with the lamp in his hand. He carefully looks forward at the uneven passage in the dim light of the lamp and reaches the place where the king of meditators, with his hair in coils sits in the lotus pose. His massive body is dry and appears like a mere skeleton; his features seem sharp and his face is lit with an extraordinary aura. Shankar feels as if the great *yogi*, Mahadev (Lord Shiva) himself is seated. He gets so lost in the supreme emotions of devotion that tears of joy flow from his eyes. With folded hands, he begins to pray to the *guru*. Sankar's resounding voice echoes in the cave, dissolving the astonishment of the ages, "Lord! O Lord, incarnation of the most primitive God, I bow to you. You are the cobra-hooded bed, on whom Lord Vishnu rests. You are the adornment of Shiva. You are holding this earth with all the seas and mountains. You have adopted this human form so that man may not fear your one-thousand hood. I know you are the real Patanjali. I seek shelter at your lotus feet with the desire to attain the ultimate knowledge."

Shankar's vigorous heart-rending voice draws the aged ascetics to enter the cave. With their hearts beating in the dim light of the lamp, they see that the child-monk is so absorbed in salutation of the *guru* that he does not notice the vibrations in the *guru's* body. Everyone looks with awe that the *guru* has left meditation and opened his eyes. Seeing the *guru* awake, everyone rejoices with bowed heads and prostrate before him. What a wonderful sight! On one side is the founder of the *Yogasutra* commentator, the *mahayogi*, the Patanjali, and on the other is Shankar from far south, rising like a sun on the banks of the Narmada. With the arrival of a young monk, Mahayogi Govindapada awakens from his millennium-old meditation to return to the earth. News about the *guru* breaking his meditation spreads in all four directions and the *guru's* cave now becomes a site for pilgrimage.

Guru Govindapada has accepted the young monk as his disciple. The cave has now become the centre of learning, where many saints along with the child-monk gather to acquire knowledge.

□

16
Kumbha Parable

Even in the searing summer heat, it is cool and green on the Narmada coast, while the whole world is ablaze at the appearance of Sun-god above the river-bed. Humans, while hesitant, wear some clothes to observe social rites, but there is no such bond for trees, who shed their leaves unhesitatingly. From the fields and the plains to the heights of the hills, the entire earth is burning like a hot furnace. Householders consider it advisable to spend the afternoon inside their homes in towns and cities, but the Govindapada Ashram presents a different scene. Guru Govindapada sits in his customary lotus pose, lost in deep meditation and observing *samadhi* while the rest of the *ashram* hums with activity. Somewhere a *hathayogi* practices the head-stand despite the scorching heat of sunlight, while another considers the sunlight too weak as he is drenched with sweat on being seated in front of the burning fire, lighted with dung cakes. As far as the eyes can see, something bizarre and super human seems to be happening. When the heat reaches its peak, the Rain-god, Indra, spreads dark black clouds over the sky, making everyone happy as they enjoy the shower of raindrops after the dust-filled storm.

Due to the daily showers, the heat begins to lose its intensity, marking the onset of the monsoon. Now it rains with full vigour. Lush greenery and flowing water dominate the landscape. Since the last fifteen days rain has not taken a break even for a day. Continuous rain has transformed small streams into flowing rivers. What to say about the rivers? The flowing water from all directions enters River Narmada which overflows to enter the sea.

Narmada is a river of vigour and beauty. Its water level rises higher and higher. The deluge is now indifferent to the flow; even to the banks. Huge trees flow like minor straws in the sweeping waters. The villagers who live near the banks are seen rushing to high dunes and hills to save their lives. Wild animals run astray with uncontrolled fear as they notice the water rushing to the entrance of the cave like a furious lioness. The distraught disciples are worried about the safety of their *guru* who is engrossed in his meditation in this cave, oblivious to the world outside. The disciples cannot leave their *guru* as they fear that in the next few moments, their death in water is inevitable. The disciples with concern writ large on their faces notice Shankar placing an earthen pot at the entrance of the cave.

"What good will such a small pitcher do, friend?" one asks.

The other remarks, "Shankar, we need to awaken the *guru* from his meditation and guide him to a safe place. What game are youplaying with this small pitcher?"

Shankar replies calmly, "My friends, just as Sage Agastya swallowed the ocean, similarly my pitcher will drink all the water of the flood."

With disbelief and awestruck eyes, the disciples notice the flood waters receding on touching the pitcher.

"Miracle! This is a miracle!" shout the disciples in joy and admiration.

"No... no, this is due to the blessings of the *guru* and the blessings of the holy Mother Narmada."

Shankar very humbly refuses to take the credit and says, "*Guru* has taught this to me. This is due to his glory; not mine."

The Narmada waters recede as fast as they had risen. *Guru's* meditation remains uninterrupted while his disciples sit down to meditate. Several days later, when the *guru* becomes conscious of the world around, the disciples narrate to him the entire story.

The *guru* had happily connected with Shankar in his heart. He extends his hand towards Shankar's head to bless him, "Shankar, you are no longer to work for yourself, but for the world. You are the one for whom I was waiting. Your arrival has proved true the prophecy of my visionary *guru*, Shri Gaudapada. Son, just as you accommodated the overflowing waters of the Narmada in a small earthen pot, similarly for the welfare of the world, you should spread the composite meaning of the *Vedas* in one *Brahmasutra* commentary. This is my blessing as well as my command."

□

17

Guru's Order for Departure

Shankar had completed four years of learning in the *ashram*. The *guru* had taught him the *hathayoga* in the first year and *rajayoga* in the second. With the completion of *hathayoga* and *rajayoga*, Shankar had acquired supernatural powers. Now he could hear distant conversations and see distant sites. He could travel long distances in the blink of an eye, enter anyone's body and return to his own body. Even self-desired death was in his control now. In the third year, the *guru* had taught him the *gyanyoga* and the mysteries of hearing, contemplation, meditation, perception and *samadhi*. Now Shankar was becoming cosmic from mundane; he now began to radiate with the light of God. He was no longer a physical body but a divine being. Delighted with the progress of the disciple, Govindapada asks Shankar, one day, "Son, I have taught you everything. Are you still curious to learn anything else?"

"No, *gurudev*, by your grace, all my doubts have been cleared; now, I feel enlightened more than ever. If you grant me permission, I would like to work towards receiving salvation! "

"No Shankar, at this moment, don't think of your salvation. You have to restore truth and religion for the salvation of millions of people. For now, relinquish your personal interest and worry about the other creatures. You are born for this; make your birth meaningful. Son, I have been waiting for you since ages as per the orders of my *guru*. The central postulation is the identity of the self (*atman*) with Brahman, thus defending the liberating knowledge of the self. The doctrine of Advaita Vedanta is a Hindu philosophy which focuses on Brahman, *atman* (soul), *vidya* (knowledge), *avidya* (ignorance), *maya* (wealth), *karma* (action) and *moksha* (salvation). The Indian sub-continent, which is popularly known as Jambudweep, has been suffering from all klinds of ills over the ages. To bring about its purgation, I have been in deep meditation. Now, after giving you knowledge, I have become free. From here, you should depart for Kashi to visit Lord Vishwanath, who will pave the path for your future life."

Shankar humbly followed the orders of the *guru* and starts preparing for the journey to Kashi.

He departs from his *guru's* cave, bubbling with energy of reverence and faith. While inquiring the way to Kashi, he and his fellow-monks move away from the banks of Rievr Narmada. After several days of hiking, they reach Benaras on the banks of River Ganga.

□

18

Benaras – The City of Nine *Rasas*

Benaras, the city of the nine *rasas,* is the capital of devotion and knowledge. Benaras is home to all kinds of beliefs and disbeliefs and to different schools of thoughts. Even the wisest of scholars has often suffered defeat among the challenges faced here.

Lord Vishwanath is not merely seated here, he resides here. One after the other, great debates have taken place here. The temples in Benaras are as many as the waves in River Ganga.

It is said that Benaras lies on the trident of Shiva. One after the other, renowned teachers, educators, reformers, *gurus, tirthankaras* and Bodhisattvas have come here and returned enchanted after tasting the *navrasas* of Benaras. Not only the residents of Kashi (Benaras), even the pilgrims arriving from elsewhere get hypnotised by the divine and invisible charm of Shankar. A devout boy named Sanandan from remote Chola dynasty has taken shelter under him. He had the strong urge to take ascetic initiation from the teenage monk Shankar, his *guru*.

On seeing Sanandan, Shankar gets so enchanted that he persuades him to become a monk. Sanandan becomes his first disciple. Thereafter there has been a flux of regular disciples, though there is none like Sanandan. Sanandan is devoted deeply to his *guru* and seems like a shadow of his *guru*. Hence, the other disciples have named him as *Guru's* Hanuman.

□

19

Devi-*Darshan*

Shankar is on his way to Manikarnika Ghat for his daily bath in the wee hours of the morning. It is still dark due to the absence of dawn's light. In the middle of the narrow road, leading to the *ghat*, a young woman is seen weeping while keeping the corpse of her dead husband on her lap. The monks' congregation halts, waits for some time for her to move, but with no other way out, Shankar request her, "Mother, if you were to put the corpse aside, we will be able to go to the *ghat*."

The grief-stricken girl does not hear anything, but keeps wailing. When Shankar requests again, she says, "O monk, why don't you say to the corpse to get aside?"

On hearing this, Shankar says, "Mother, you say so because you are in deep mourning. How can the dead body be removed on its own?"

"O meditator, you consider the absolute Brahman to be the creator of the world, then with Shakti, why can't the dead body be removed?"

Shankar is stunned at this response of the woman. When he closes his eyes for a moment, he realises that he is in the company of *Mahamaya Adi Shakti*, Mother Bhagwati. Goddess Bhagwati's veneration flows out from his throat and he sees with dilated eyes that there is no corpse on the path now and there is no woman either; everything has disappeared. After taking a bath with a happy heart, he realises the truth of the inseparability of the soul and Brahma.

He is now basking in the advanced peak of spirituality and feels blissful, so much so that anyone who meets him feels that meeting him is like taking a dip in the holy waters of the Ganga of joy. The knowledge gained on the banks of the Narmada have fructified on the banks of River Ganga.

□

20

Shiva-*Darshan*

The streets of Benaras have their own flavour.They are curved and narrow, becoming formless from corporeal to take shape again. Shankar goes through these lanes to bathe in the Ganga, where the people of Benaras leave the path meant for sages and move aside, but today this does not happen.

Shankar and his disciples notice in front of them stands an untidy, stout and unholy outcast holding the leash of four massive dogs. It is clear from his arrogance that he is not inclined to give way to the monks.

Shankar is constrained to say, "Hey outcast, move to one side and give us way, so that we can go."

But why was he going to obey? Seeing him deaf to his words, Shankar says in a slightly louder voice, "Oh, wait! Hold back your dogs. Let us go."

The ugly and defiant *chandala* asks Shankar in pure Sanskrit, "Who are you asking to move away? The soul or the body? The soul is omnipresent, passive and pure. If you are asking the body to move away, then the body is inert – how can it move? Then what is the difference between my body and yours? Is there any difference between a Brahmin and a *chandala* from a basic point of view? What is the difference between the sun reflected in the Ganga waters and the sun reflected in wine? Hey! What type of ultimate knowledge do you possess? In which *Veda* is the concept of untouchability given that separates human beings? When the soul and the Supreme Soul are one, how can there be any discrimination between souls?"

Shankar is struck dumb at the intellectual rhetoric of the *chandala* and is forced to maintain silence. He enters into meditation for a moment and on opening his eyes, finds Lord Maheshwara seated in front of him. Couplets spring out in praise of Mahadev from the throat of an emotionally-charged Shankar. He feels Maheshwara's blessings on his head and hears the Lord say, "Son, it is my command that you should re-establish the Vedic religion in this world, refute the delusions, ostentations, differences and bind all in one thread of Advaita by composing a commentary on Vyasa's *Brahmasutra* for the general public and connect it with the Ultimate Knowledge!"

Hearing this, Shankar, with a happy mind returns to the material aspect of life. There was neither a *chandala* nor a dog anywhere. His enchanted heart keeps thinking as to what kind of *leela* was this? Then he remembers the last conversation with his *guru* in the cave on the banks of Narmada, "Shankar, you go to Kashi, where you will find Lord Vishwanath.He will pave the way for your future life."

So Lord Vishwanath had visited him. After taking a bath in the Ganga, Shankar decides to go to the Badrika Ashram to compose his commentary on *Brahmasutra*! "My greetings to Vishwanath! Greetings to Devi Annapurna!"

After midnight, this group of teenage monks from Benaras set out towards the Himalayas in the shade of the twinkling stars.

□

21

The Himalayas, the Land of Penance

Moving rapidly towards the land of deities – the Himalayas – the monks reach Haridwar on the banks of River Ganga.

'Haridwar' means the 'gate of God'. Shankar feels Haridwar truly is the gateway to God. In the lush green sky-kissing canopy of trees in the Himalayan valley, the monks had visited the various place of worship and other holy sites of the city, resting and again visiting. They take a holy dip in the River Ganga and proceed ahead towards the city of sages, known as Rishikesh. Now the plain land begins to give way to hills, making the monks climb in right earnest. They reach the Yajneshwar temple established by the sages in Rishikesh where silence reigns. There is no idol, no system of worship and no visitors. Shankar camps here and the local people come to meet the teenage monks; even the priests of the temple who were hesitant initially, hasten towards them.

After seeing Shankar from close quarters, they become emotional. Within two days, a huge crowd gathers which has to be managed by the intervention of monks who come forward to help.

Shankar inquires about the whereabouts of the idol in that temple. The priest tells that his late father had hidden the idol of God in the holy Ganga to protect it against attacks by Chinese bandits. So even after an intense search, the idol could not be located anywhere, thus rendering this ancient and holy temple deserted.

Acharya Shankar asks, "If by the grace of God, that holy idol is found and is installed again, will the local society take the responsibility of worshipping it?"

On receiving everyone's consent, Shankar sits down in a meditative posture. The devotees also sit down eagerly around him. After a few moments, Shankar stands up with his eyes open and walks towards River Ganga; the rest follow behind him. After walking a few steps on the banks of the river, he indicates to the people to search at a particular spot. The devotees take a dip in the waters and one of them emerges with the idol held aloft. The atmosphere reverberates with cheers. The people are convinced that it is a miracle and reverently prostrate at Shankar's feet. Shankar raises them from the ground and on an auspicious day and at an auspicious time, the idol is established at Rishikesh. The news of this miracle performed by a teenage monk spreads far and wide.

The calm and detached young monk reaches Vidur, making his way through Laxman Jhoola towards the dense forests, to reach the *ashram* of Sage Vyas. Shankar and his disciples get overwhelmed to behold the holy confluence of Alaknanda and Bhagirathi at Devprayag, which is a city of temples. A holy dip at the confluence of Alaknanda and Bhagirathi along with ritualistic prayers at various temples of Ram-Sita, Shiva-Parvati, Ganesh, etc. fill the heart of the monks with unbound enthusiasm.

□

22

No to Human Sacrifice!

The monks move from Devprayag to reach Bilb Kedar and are now proceeding towards Srinagar, where a serious crisis and a difficult challenge awaits them.

Srinagar, the ancient capital of Uttarakhand, is famous for its temples of Kamleshwar Shiva and Lord Vishnu, but now the five Siddha centres are dominated by occultists. Their supremacy runs to such an extent that they even offer human sacrifices. What is more, no one has the courage to stop them!

At the arrival of teenage monks, the occultists are filled with pleasure and are all the more eager to please Chamunda by offering heads of these teenagers as flowers. This urge among the occultists disappears like a straw in the storm under the hypnosis of Shankar. An enlightened Shankar defeats them in a debate just as a mighty lion, the king of the forest, defeats the deer. When he asks the occultists, "Gentlemen, Mother Goddess is life-giving; how can she be pleased with the blood of her own children?"

The occultists are struck dumb and have no reply to offer. They surrender before Shankar. In the midst of the resounding cheers of the local people, he picks up the slaughter-stone and throws it into the river. After rendering Srinagar free from danger, he and his friends light the flame of spirituality and move forward to the pilgrimage centres of Rudraprayag, Nandaprayag and then to the Badri region. They spend the night in the temple of Lord Vashishteshwar in the meditative land of Vashishta at the beautiful confluence of Mandakini and Alaknanda. They resume their journey early next morning, making their first stop at Virheshwar Mahadev temple on the banks of Virahi Ganga. Distraught at the separation from Sati, Shiva's land of meditation was charged with energy where all the monks sit down to meditate. In the divine presence of the Himalayas, Shankar rejoices at the sight of the sky-kissing *deodar* trees. At the same time, the *deodars* of the Himalays aouse in his consciousness the memory of the clumps of coconut trees at Kaladi. After crossing the Garuda Ganga, the monks reach Jyotirdham.

The king himself is present here to welcome him. He requests Shankar to stay on for some days to give his people and him religious enlightenment. The devotional spirit and hospitality of the hill people is successful in persuading Shankar to prolong his stay here.

Every day, men and women flock from the surrounding villages in their colourful clothes to visit and offer their prayers to Shankar. Among them, there is no dearth of scholars or Brahmins either. The crowd increases day by day on hearing Sankar's wonderful commentaries on the *Upanishads*, the *Bhagavad Gita* and the *Brahmasutras*.

Every day there is a beautiful sight to behold. Its strangeness lies in the fact that while the disciples are old, the *guru* is a young Shankar, a monk sitting in the posture of knowledge. He himself is a form of bliss.The disorder among the devotees gets replaced with calm discipline on catching a glimpse of the monk. Every particle of Jyotirdham gets illumined with a new light. The effect of this divine congregation is seen everywhere. Shankar has a goal in his mind – after re-consecrating the Jyotirdham, he has to reach the land of meditation of Nar and Narayan, the Badridham via Vishwaprayag, Chhoti Ganga, Brahmakund, Vishnukund, Ganesh Tirtha and Pandukeshwar.

□

23

Re-establishment of Badrinarayana

With Shankar's arrival, there is a festive gaiety in Badridham on the banks of River Alaknanda. Taking a bath in the Tapt Kund adjacent to the temple, when they go to pay a visit to Badrinarayan, Shankar and his fellow disciples are bewildered to see the abandoned altar in the sanctum sanctorum of the temple. Saligram is enshrined the sanctorum instead of the idol. When the astonished Acharya comes out after offering his prayers, the priest of the temple approaches him and says, "Our ancestors, who were attacked by Chinese bandits, had hidden the idol of the deity in this pool, but even after countless efforts to find it we could not find it. Being compelled, we are now worshipping Saligram (a particular type of stone worshipped as Vishnu) as God."

Acharya, in a serious yet a balanced voice, asks, "If the deity can be found again, will you be prepared to restore it?"

Everyone eagerly agrees.

At this, Acharya turns and starts descending towards the Narad Kund, but the priests stop him, saying, "Lord, do not enter this pool as many of our dear persons have lost their lives. No one has returned from it; please don't go."

But Shankar, fearless and unshakable, descends into the pool, takes a dip and comes out with the idol to the surprise of the people gathered around. After consecrating the idol on the altar, Acharya Shankar appoints one of his reliable and accomplished disciples as a priest. The entire population of Badridham prostrates at his feet with reverence. There is unprecedented joy in Badridham due to the re-consecration of the deity in this abandoned temple. The sound of the devotees chanting begins to echo in the area.

Acharya establishes Lord Badrinarayan in the temple according to the rules laid down in the scriptures. He entrusts the responsibility of conducting the rites and rituals the chosen disciple and proceeds towards Vyas Ashram.

□

24

During the Himalayan Tour

Acharya Shankar needs solitude to compose his commentary. Such solitude is possible only in the inaccessible Himalayas. The ancient Vyas Ashram is the most suitable place to write the commentary on the *Brahmasutra* of the great Sage Ved Vyas. The *Mahabharata* was also composed by Vyas in this hermitage.

Moving towards this historical and holy place, Acharya becomes emotional on noticing the white snow-capped peaks all around. The beauty of Alaknanda combined with that of Keshav Ganga is breathtaking. Here, at Keshavprayag, at the confluence of the two rivers, temple bells resonate only on festivals. There is pure and unhindered peace here.

The dense fog is so thick that even the Sun-god does not disturb the peace of this place. While bathing in the ice-cold water at the confluence in Keshavprayag, Acharya notices a large cave on the left side, at the foot of a huge mountain.

He proceeds towards the cave with his disciples. The cave is a huge natural habitat in the chest of the mountain. Possibly before the advent of civilisation the place was a refuge for the primitive man!

The young monks set up their camp here. Protection from the icy winds, the fatigue and labour of travelling begin to disappear in the warmth of the cave.

□

25

Vyas Cave – Sanandan

An amazing energy is witnessed in Vyas cave. Here the *guru* remains mostly engrossed in meditation and when he wakes up from it, he remains immersed in reading, contemplating and meditating on the *Brahmasutra*. His disciples too experience new heights of spirituality at this place.

After a deep contemplative study, the *guru* is seen writing the commentary. Now, he composes the commentary daily and teaches the new compositions to the disciples; the disciples feel obliged. From Acharya's commentary, they are able to understand the meaning of the esoteric verses of *Brahmasutra.*

The dear disciple Sanandan receives special affection from his *acharya*. This disturbs the minds of other disciples. Envy by the human mind raises its head even in the spiritual waves caused by the holy atmosphere inside the Vyas cave. Acharya has to treat this, else even minor troubles can assume serious proportions and cause trouble.

One day Sanandan goes across the Alaknanda in search of tuber roots and fruits. Meanwhile Acharya is engrossed in replying to questions raised by the disciples when all of a sudden Sanandan is seen walking towards them.

Acharya calls out to him, "Sanandan! Sanandan, come soon."

The bridge is far away. On hearing Acharya's voice, Sanandan begins to walk briskly over the raging river. On the other side, the disciples are shocked at this frightening sight. The fierce and leaping waves of the Alaknanda are so forceful as to carry away even an elephant, like a straw in the wind. Oh God! Sanandan's life is in peril!

Acharya smiles and consoles his disciples, "Don't worry, nothing will happen to Sanandan."

The distraught disciples look at him with awe-struck eyes. Nothing does really happen to Sanandan. He is seen joyfully running over the river as if a bridge has been laid under his feet! Acharya smiles and within a few moments, Sanandan comes running to his *guru*. The onlookers stand rooted to the spot. Unbelievable! But how could this have happened right in front of their eyes. Acharya chides Sanandan with affection and compassion, "What was the need to jump into the raging river? You should have come over the bridge."

Sanandan looks back and sees the torrenting Alaknanda and realises that he had jumped into the river, losing control over his mind at the call of his *guru*. With his mind focused on his *guru's* call, how could he think of the path he was taking? But he did not drown in the current of the river. He recalled that wherever he had set his foot, he had felt the petals of a cool tufted lotus! Charged with emotion, Sanandan chants, "*Guru kripa kevalam*" and prostrates at the feet of the *guru*. The smiling Acharya notices his disciples' faces glowing with wonder in place of jealousy. Acharya lifts up Sanandan affectionately and says, "Sanandan, from today your name will be Padmapada."

In the serene solitude of the Himalayan cold white snow, Acharya Shankar's hermitage buzzes with activity as the can be seen reading, learning, dialogue-analysing and discussing. Acharya is busy composing the commentary on *Brahmasutra*, the *Upanishad, Bhagavad Gita* and *Vishnu Sahastranama.*

The crowd of devotees increases day by day during his long stay in the Badri region. As soon as the composition of the commentary gets over, Acharya desires to leave Jyotirdham to go Kedar. This is the impr e ssion already gathered by his disciples and therefore they get busy with the preparations for his journey, rest and welcome.

Chanting *"Om namah Shivaya"*, Acharya and the monks move towards Kedar and reach Tungnath. Not only is this pilgims' team mesmerised at the wonderful natural beauty of Tungnath, but Acharya Shankar himself is taken in by the calm and cool surroundings. He experiences non-dualism here and feels one with Nature. The same is the experience of the disciples.

Enjoying the experience of Almighty's power in the ocean of ecstasy, this family of ascetics descends from the slopes of the mountains and reaches Gauri Kund, the place where Goddess Parvati had performed penance. Here they get refreshed by taking a dip in the warm waters of the pond.

After a few days of rest in the warm ambience of Gauri Kund, these tireless travellers move on, climbing the hills to visit Kedarnath. Despite feeling cold due to the snow all around and with difficulty in breathing, no one stops as the goal is to reach Kedarnath before darkness descends.

After bowing and meditating before Lord Kedarnath, when Shankar opens his eyes, he finds his disciples shivering in extreme cold. In this wide expanse of snow, the icy wind pierces through the bones like sharp arrows, making them shiver.

Acharya again meditates for a few moments and notices a spring of hot water near the temple. On his orders, after seeing this geyser spewing hot water when the place in excavated, the disciples present are surprised and cheer him loudly. Acharya again resorts to meditation. After completing his penance in Kedarnath till the next full moon, Acharya continues his journey towards Gangotri. His desire to see Bhagirathi is so strong that he forgets the travails of the journey over the inaccessible path.

The dense forests and fierce wild animals had been his companions since childhood. Avalanches and landslides are the new hurdles that Acharya experiences but he is undeterred by them.

□

26

Vyas Cave (Gangotri)

Not only Shankar, even his disciples have learned to ignore the sufferings, finding solace and comfort in the cool shadow of their *guru*. This group of young monks, used to rigorous austerity, marches forward unaffected by the hardships on the journey.

Acharya is held spellbound as soon as he gets a first glimpse of the wondrous beauty of the soothing waves of Bhagirathi Ganga in the uninhabited peace of the white snow-peaks of the Himalayas. His poetic soul comes to life and from his melodious voice spring the praise of River Ganga: "O god, who is purgatory of the three worlds, who melts the flow like a generous stream, one who resides in the hair locks of Shiva as the pious Ganga, may my mind reside at your lotus feet."

This beautiful verse known as the *'Ganga stuti'* emerging from the divine voice of Acharya blesses the disciples. After paying a visit, the disciples along with Acharya return to Gangotri.

Acharya orders the ruler of Jyotirdham to construct a temple for Goddess Ganga in Gangotri so that the ordinary pilgrims may not have to undertake the life-threatening journey to Gomukh. The devout king enthusiastically orders the construction of the temple.

□

27

Vyas Cave (Order for Debate and Victory)

After the Gangotri stay, Acharya and his disciples reach the place of penance – Uttar Kashi. In this ancient centre of pilgrimage, the divine touch of the Ganga running towards the north renders the atmosphere more pious. Acharya seems to be at a loss of his physical identity on arriving at this place. He now finds his body acting as a barrier. He becomes so anxious to be one with the Supreme Being that even the body is no longer acceptable. On seeing this, the disciples become worried. They cannot ever imagine separation from their beloved *guru*.

Moving beyond the body, Acharya's consciousness knows that with the completion of the sixteenth year of his body, he will absorb himself in the Supreme Being, Brahma. The drop has to immerse in the ocean to reach beyond the sensation of hunger, thirst, sleep and rest.

Moving forward on the journey to the Infinite, he utters a melodious poem, "I am Brahma."

Acharya's mind is inclined towards the Infinite. To keep it connected with the world, the anxious disciples pray to Acharya to teach them the commentary that is still left. Acharya begins to lecture. The disciples are convinced that the Acharya would remain on earth till the lectures continue.

One morning, while teaching the formula for maintaining the physique, Acharya notices an elderly but glowing Brahmin guest. Acharya welcomes him and gives him a seat. The guest is neither interested in the reception nor in the seat; his interest lies in debating with Shankar. He immediately asks Acharya, "What is the meaning of the first definition of the first passage of the third chapter of Ved Vyas's *Brahmasutra*?"

A humble Shankar salutes and replies, "O Acharya, my scholarship is not worthy of pride, but I will try to answer your question." After a moment, he narrates the correct explanation of that definition. The Brahmin is astonished, yet refrains from praising the answers to his questions. Despite receiving appropriate answers, he shows no satisfaction; instead he contradicts Shankar, with the full might of his knowledge. The session continues with a series of questions, counter-questions, rebuttals and refutations. A polite Acharya remains calm and unmoved at the onslaught of thunderbolts. By giving the simplest answers to the most complex questions, he thwarts every attack with a simple enthusiasm.

In this unequal battle of knowledge, both the warriors fight with amazing might as the disciples of Acharya stare as astonished spectators. References from *Shruti*, *Smriti*, *Puranas* and *Upanishads* are used, but no one emerges victorious. Knowing that sun is about to set, the guest adjourns the debate for the day and takes leave.

The next day, followed by the next day; the debate continues unabated like this for seven days. On the evening of the seventh day, the Brahmin goes away after suspending the theological debates.

Prior to this night, Padmapada had asked Acharya Shankar, "Lord it's my curiosity which is troubling me. Is it possible that this unique Brahmin, aged in wisdom, could possibly be Ved Vyas himself?"

A pleased Acharya replies, "Yes, I too feel the same way."

"But Lord, how is that possible?" Padmapada counters.

"It is possible, Padmapada! Remember, I told you that

Maharishi Ved Vyas is one of the seven great men who are immortal and still exists in the present creation. Anyway, I'll ask him tomorrow." Saying this, the Acharya goes to rest, while Padmapada's curiosity keeps him awake throughout the night.

The next day, the same icon of knowledge appears again but not empty handed. As soon as he arrives, he starts the debate by asking a very complicated question.

Shankar, most humbly pays obeisance to him and requests with reverence, "O sage, I will answer your question, but I pray that we would be feel blessed if you were to give your introduction. We believe that you are the great immortal sage Ved Vyas himself."

On hearing this, the guest's face lights up with a new aura. He affectionately hugs Acharya to his heart. The group of disciples is delighted to see this lovely union of wise warriors who till now had been engrossed in the verbal war of knowledge. It is a wonderful occasion where the experience of centuries embraces the enthusiasm of the present in a wonderful amalgamation of the old with the new!

With a child-like enthusiasm, Acharya Shankar shows the commentaries he has written to the sage. The sage is no less delighted on reading the purity, the excellence and the emotional depth of the commentaries.

Seeing the sage satisfied, Acharya bends down on his knees in front of the sage and requests, "Lord, according to your wishes, I have completed all the assigned duties; now I want to be free of this body through *samadhi yoga* with your blessings."

The disciples notice that the reverend Ved Vyas has turned silent for a moment and has closed his eyes. Shankar's eyes are focused only on his guest's dazzling face. He feels that the great sage has gone into *samadhi.*

After a few moments, the sage returns to his body with bright and enlightened eyes. Shankar stares at him and their eyes meet. In a strong and stable voice, the sage says, "No Shankar, your responsibilities are not yet over. By winning in the debate with various top religious persons, your work is not complete. You have to channelise your energy into the uplift of the Advaita Vedanta and the revival of culture."

"But Lord, you know, my life is over," Acharya argues.

"Yes son, on being satisfied with your work I have come here today only to give you the boon of longevity." The soft and serious words of the great Sage Ved Vyas echo in Acharya's ears. "There is a purpose in the birth of every living being in the universe, Shankar. For the fulfilment of the purpose for which you were born, the Creator has given you an additional sixteen years to live. First of all, defeat the great ritualistic Kumaril Bhatt in a debate; after that, re-establish the authority of Vedanta by roaming in this great country, extending from the Himalayas to Rameshwaram; eliminate hypocrisy, differences, evils and religious anarchy. Start on your victorious journey."

After giving this order, Ved Vyas disappears into thin air. The happiness of the disciples knows no bounds as an obedient Shankar sets out in search of Kumaril Bhatt.

The Creator had scripted in his fate to be an eternal traveller and had forgotten to write the word 'rest'.

□

28
Kumaril Parable

While entering the cool waters at the confluence where the three rivers meet called Sangam at Prayag, Shankar remembers the Purna river of his childhood. All the memories of Kaladi come flooding to his mind as soon as he takes the dip. He remembers going to the banks of River Purna by holding his mother's finger, to swim, to bathe and to return after worship. All the memories get recalled.

Shankar also remembers the love and affection of his mother, her reluctance at his renunciation, his warm tears soon mingling in the cool stream at the meeting point of the three rivers. Nobody could see and know of it.

He feels calm in his mind and in a wet body, he returns to the shore, wipes the body dry with a towel, reclines on the trunk of the tamarind tree and remains observing the flow of the confluence (*triveni*).

He decides to meet the great Kumaril Bhatt today. He is the same Kumaril, who made the Vedic religion strong during tough times through the strength of his efforts and knowledge. Kumaril's principles of *Mimamsa* are likely to prevail over everyone in the debate. Shankar has to defeat the same invincible Kumaril in the theological debate and make him the flag-bearer of Monoism.

These days, Kumaril is in Prayag, Shankar has reached Prayag city with the desire to meet his adversary for a debate. He sends one of his monks to the city to find Kumaril. Just then, Kumaril's envoy is seen coming towards Shankar, "Disaster...happening... Swami! Disaster!"

"What's the matter? Is everything not fine?" asks Shankar.

"Now how can it be fine, Lord? How can anything be perfect in a nation in which a brilliant scholar like Kumaril is planning to commit suicide?"

"But why would Kumaril commit suicide? He has a reputation for fighting against injustice and tyranny. He is not the one to give up."

"Swami, I am coming after seeing with my own eyes the preparations being made for his self-sacrifice; no one is able to stop him. He has announced to sacrifice himself in the fire."

Shankar hurriedly picks up his wooden staff and water vessel to go and meet Kumaril, along with his companions. The speed of his steps and the aura on his face could easily have prompted the crowd to make way for him, but today there is a huge crowd – from every direction men, women, elders and children are rushing on the same path in order to reach Kumaril. There are all sorts of people in the crowd, including ordinary householders as also the wealthy and respected ones. Vain scholars, serious thinkers, useless spectators, Brahmin boys, religious stakeholders of monasteries – all are making their way to that vast ground where only the head of the great teacher Kumaril Bhatt, in a fearless posture, can be seen on a huge pile of straw. The rest of his body is hidden inside a pile of flammable straw.

The crowd is crying aloud and had they not been bound by the limits of religion, they would have scattered the whole arrangement.

On the left of Kumaril are seated Brahmin boys from various institutions; on the right are present dignitaries of the city. Kumaril has rejected everyone's appeal to desist from taking such a step. According to his instructions, a fire has been lit and smoke begins to billow out, rising into the sky.

Shankar notices that the face of the Vedic philosopher Kumaril is calm and glowing with satisfaction at the thought of fulfilling his resolve. No sign of anxiety or sorrow is visible on his face.

Kumaril's face lights up with a smile as soon as he sees Shankar. This is their first meeting, but both are acquainted with each other's reputation and fame. Both are resolved to re-establish the *Vedas* even though there is a difference in their approach. The entire crowd watches with anticipation the meeting of two great men at that critical moment. Despite it being their first meeting, it seems that both have been familiar with each other since many births! Their eyes also reveal their mutual respect as they greet each other.

Shankar says in a melodious voice, "O great scholar, I have come to you at the command of reverend Ved Vyas. Why have you taken the decision to immolate yourself?"

Kumaril replies, "O greatest Brahmin, I have committed two serious sins in life – first, I defeated a Buddhist *guru* in debate and hence spoiled his life; second, I tried to prove that existence of God cannot be proved and the actions enjoined in the *Vedas* have definite results without any external interference from God. For the mitigation of these two sins, I am taking a fire-bath. Now please tell me what has bought you here?"

Shankar replies in a shocked voice, "O supreme Brahmin, I know that you have struggled throughout your life for the defeat of the slanderers of the *Vedas* and for the protection of the scriptures. I will douse this fire with water from my wooden vessel. I have written a commentary on the *Brahmasutra* for the propagation of *Mimamsa*. You must compose an explanation on my commentaries."

Kumaril's face brightens up as he says, "O best teacher, if I go back on my resolve, the benefits of religion will be violated more than me. I have been deprived of the privilege of writing the explanation on your commentaries. Even debate is not possible now, but by defeating my disciple Mandan Mishra in the debate, you can accomplish your goal."

Shankar, in a serious voice, to protect Kumaril, says, "Sir, India and its Vedic culture are being hit hard. More than foreigners, our mutual mental, ideological, religious and political conflicts are weakening this great nation of ours. At such a critical time, there is a greater need for you to live than to die and preserve the dignity of culture and religion. Ordinary public minds won't understand the moral logic behind your self-immolation and weak-hearted people may be instigated to commit suicide by this act. You can influence the nation's mind and heart by staying alive."

But the fire begins to burn Kumaril's body and limbs, while the large crowd of people listens to this heart-breaking conversation between two men with sad and defeated hearts. The resplendent Kumaril, in the flames of smoke and fire, replies, "I beg your forgiveness. I struggled throughout my youth and now this donation of my body in old age will restore the honour of the *guru* before the younger generation. At the same time, it may awaken the soul of the majority of people who are involved only in fulfilling their personal interests even at the time of the pitiable condition of the nation and culture.

"Now accept my salutations in my last moments and chant the salvation (*tarak*) *mantra* in my ears, so that I can be free of this body."

Appreciating Kumaril's firm resolve with his heart, Shankar chants the *moksha mantra*. Kumaril's body is turned to ash while the crowd praises his resolve. The feeling of collective defeat is now replaced with pride at sacrifice and martyrdom.

The story of the martyrdom of Kumaril spreads like a legend, not only from Prayag to the entire *Aryavarta*, but also to the seashores of the far south to distant lands.

In the far south of India, Kumaril is considered an incarnation of Skanda, the son of Shiva, while North India is proud of him in its own way to claim him a Brahmin of Mithila. Western India remains true to the Vedic values through his vigorous efforts while the newly built *chaityas* in B ihar and the *stupas* of the Buddhists are unable to wipe away the ancient Vedic beliefs. The discussion on Kumari's courage, st r uggle, knowledge, sacrifice in all directions – east, west, north and south – serves as a new lifeline for this ancient religion. In *gurukuls*, Brahmin boys are told stories about Kumaril and how he gave borth to a national religion and everlasting culture at the cost of sacrificing his own life. Kumaril lived like a warrior and went to heaven like a warrior.

Gautam Buddha had tried to remove the shortcomings that had developed over time in Vedic religion, but then, over time, his own disciples had got infected with the same germ of personal ego, hypocrisy and selfishness, for which he had to struggle throughout his life to remove. This mishap has recurred in every period of history of the world when disciples and followers have often become the greatest destroyers of the principles of their religious *guru* and leader.

The polytheism of Vedic religion was later accepted as a defect and Gautam Buddha strongly opposed it, but his disciples created innumerable forms of Bodhisattvas. Gautam Buddha spoke against incarnation but could not save himself from becoming an incarnation. The new religion of non-violence turned violent with the support of power. The Buddha's message of kindness and compassion now survives only in the Jataka tales.

Gautam Buddha's sharp wisdom in preachings dimmed after his departure and his disciples could spread only his simple messages with religious fervour throughout the world, but could not stop the pollution that had entered Buddhism. When vested interests entered Buddhist monasteries in the same way as *ashrams* of monks and sages, the public began to turn to Vedic religion. Kumaril Bhatt became the voice of this resistance.

Kumaril was well versed in grammar, *nirukta* and the *Vedas*. His nonpareil talent had been chiseled by *guru's* grace in such a way that his speech had become the divine word and his sentences become the *Veda's* sentences. Whoever listened, became his and took refuge in the *Vedas*.

His study and contemplation had only one purpose – to convey the simple, intuitive message of the *Vedas* to the common man. This act of Kumaril created an upheaval among the local Buddhists, but none could win over him in debate. There was none among the young Buddhists with as deep a knowledge as he and none was as sharp as he among the senior Buddhists. His fame and knowledge of the *Vedas* began to spread day by day.

Dharmakirti ll, a young monk from the Sarnath Buddhist monastery had been educated at Nalanda. He was equally great in name and fame. Debates between Vedists and Buddhists took place frequently in which Dharmakirti's victory kept the flag of fame running high by his winning every debate, but now the competition was with the indomitable Kumaril.

As soon as the debate began, Kumaril attacked the *Vedas* and the *Shrutis* with such precision that the arguments on religion met the same fate as a deer caught in the claws of a lion. On getting defeated, Dharmakirti ll admitted that he had been defeated by logic and not because of the superiority of Vedic religion. "If you had lived in Nalanda with Buddhist principles like me, then you would have understood the basic religion; at present it's not in your capacity."

The arrow hit the right target. Kumaril was hurt even after emerging victorious and Dharamkirti committed suicide owing to the guilt of defeat that defamed him. Kumaril, in his heart of hearts, was hurt by Dharmakirti's satire, but no solution could strike his mind. His fame had spread so far and wide that it was not possible to enter Nalanda through his name and image. Who would allow an enemy to enter the fort and without entering Nalanda, Kumaril's goal could not be fulfilled!

"The thing which is to be prohibited can be denied only when it is known, not otherwise." Night and day he kept thinking: निषेध्यबोधाबद्धि–निषेध्यबाध: ।

The enthusiasm of the Buddhists gave way to aggression on receiving shelter from the state. They condemned the vices present in Vedic religion. The hierarchical caste system, the huge expenses spent on rituals, the greed and wiliness of some of the priests were the issues of discontent in the society. The Buddhists ignited sparks of discontent with intelligence, which gradually turned into raging flames. The authority of status quo collapsed in the face of the courage, rationality, generosity and action of the Buddhists.

The merits of Vedic religion became its faults over a period of time. The unparalleled religious freedom with not one central and universally-accepted religious sermoniser turned into religious anarchy with changing times. Innumerable religious sermonisers sprang up in villages with independent religious rulers and their fanatical disciples targeting each other's throats.

The united and invincible India was now divided into innumerable small states – princely states; in which no one was under anyone; each had his own sovereignty.

The *varna* system, which was initially work-based, in which each one had the freedom to choose his occupation and career according to his will and ability, was now encroached upon by the fungus of vested interests. Craftsmanship was looked down upon, while warriors and priests became omnipotent. Proficiency in earning and saving money was no longer a matter of honour, but of hatred. Traders and shopkeepers became the target of envy. The new religion seemed like a breath of fresh air to the afflicted, who began to take shelter under the Buddha–'*Buddam sharanam gacchami*'. Village after village started to get initiated into this new religion.

The tension in the minds of these new Buddhists harbouring wrong attitudes that they had acquired from the old religion made them more aggressive and bitter. They openly told the people, "This king is on our side, so you guys better adopt this new path." Opportunists also started joining the new state religion.

Puffed with pride at their success, the Buddhist religious leaders roamed across the country, condemning the *Vedas*. They termed the ideological generosity and intellectual freedom of the *Vedas* as absurdity. A few greedy and indecent priests came to be presented as the symbols of Vedic religion. They were ridiculed while the *Vedas, Shruti, Puranas* and the desire to learn were mocked at.

After the initial popularity and widespread dominance as a reformist movement, the self-confident and frenzied Buddhists began to divide among themselves. They took the orthodox form in this new religion and new sect. They themselves became victims of all those faults against which Tathagata had initiated his struggle.

The emergence of *tantra-mantra*, worship-ritualism, witchcraft, bodily pleasure, violence and sinful acts in the name of the new religion created disillusionment among the people. Faith in the Vedic path began to return again on receiving a favourable environment. Against this background, Kumaril and people like him raised their head through intellect and concerted efforts. They held the firm belief in the benign authenticity and spiritual depth of Vedanta, but they wanted to prove its superiority through facts and arguments in open debates, not through power and craftiness. Dharmakirti's challenge was echoing in Kumaril's He decided that no matter how, but he had to go to Nalanda to study Buddhism thoroughly and then travel across the country to present a factual rebuttal.

□

29

Nalanda, Pilgrimage of Knowledge

Nalanda, famous as a seat of learning and science, is the dream of everyone who has love and thirst for knowledge. Getting into Nalanda University is as arduous as going to heaven with one's body. Brilliant and stubborn students from all over the world have queued outside the massive gates of this great centre of learning for years. Thousands of students study here, but a large majority of them returns disappointed every year when not allowed admission.

The difficult process of admission includes fine sieving of every candidate out of whom only one or two succeed in getting through. Here introduction, influence, wealth, modesty, solicitation are considered faults. The only measure of admission is the ability of the student and the capital of his studies which are contemplation and reverence for Buddhism.

Kumaril was not devoid of study and contemplation and made all efforts to hide his disrespect towards Buddhism. He got through all the stages of the difficult entrance examination skilfully and entered Nalanda, the great fortress of Buddhists.

The sky-kissing giant university of Nalanda is a unique example of architecture. Ten thousand students here immerse themselves in studying and researching in subjects like Buddhism, Vedic religion, philosophy, medicine, grammar, economics, mathematics, etc. The spacious complex has well-planned gardens, pathways, galleries, balconies, study rooms and accommodation as also grand libraries. Regular congregational prayers are held in front of the magnificent statue of Gautam Buddha. In the long and spacious food complex, there are huge stoves and food stores!

The entrance examination for the students is held at the huge entrance gate of the temple. Successful students get to experience a different world on getting admission into this university where nothing is miniscule; everything is immense, enormous!

The complex of thousands of acre consists of innumerable buildings, attics and temples. The grand residential complexes have innumerable rooms and common rooms for shower. When the stoves are lit in the large food complexes, large clouds of smoke are seen billowing towards the sky as if a ladder has been made for them to move from the earth into space.

For the operation of such a grand system, the revenue from hundreds of villages reaches the management of Nalanda. The rich people from hundreds of adjacent villages participate in the special rituals religiously and provide financial aid and grants by way of money, property, grains, etc.

Kumaril modestly follows the rules and regulations of the place and remains immersed in the study of Buddhist religion. The other students participate in sports, entertainment, painting and sculpture, etc. in their free time after their studies, but Kumaril remains focused on his goal.

Day and night, asleep or awake, Kumaril is engrossed in comprehending the principles of Buddhism. In the time left after consulting the teachers, he gets engrossed in the library. The staff in the library have started recognising him and the books he wants are readily identified and offered to him. Apart from reading in various languages about the life of Gautam Buddha, he goes through the religious scriptures, like *Tripitaka's Mahaparinirvan Sutra,* collections of *Mahayana, Collective Abhidharma, Abhidharma Gyan Prasthan* by Katyayan, *Abhidharma Kosha, Yoga Karyabhoomi Shastr a, Mahapragya Paramita Sutra, Avatayasak Sutra, Samyukta Bh umidharma Hridayashastra, Vibhasha Sutra* one by one.

What a library Nalanda has – an ocean of knowledge! Kumaril is the big fish in this ocean. Day and night, he remains deeply embedded in study, meditation and analysis. He finds that Buddhism has many sub-sections of religious scriptures. The first section of Buddha's teachings is known as *sutras;* the second section is *Geyas*; the third comprises grammar and the fourth deals with *gathas*, contains *mantras* and poems. The fifth section has a simple commentary while the sixth is popular as *Itivrittikal.* The literature pertaining to the previous births of Buddha is given in the *Jataka* section and the eighth contains literature on the extended *sutras.* The ninth volume is called *Adbhut Dharma*. It has books on the fables of miracles performed by the Buddha.

The knowledge-thirsty Kumaril absorbs and grasps the contents in the respective Buddhist texts from all these sections. He learns the four Buddhist *Agamas – Deerghagam, Madhyamagam, Samyuktagam* and *Eko Tarikagam*. He regularly recites the '*Maladevi Singh nada sutra*'. He has even read *Het Vidya Shastra* and *Shabd Vidya Shastra*. Presently he lays his hands on *Tattva Sandesh Shastra* and from next month his target is to equip himself with *Abhidharma Shastra.* While reading, Kumaril's eyes get tired but his enthusiasm does not wane.

In Nalanda, he is not just studying the religious texts but he is also analysing the conduct of Buddhist religious leaders, scholars and monks. He finds that some monks are really pure and pious. Their clothes and conduct are spotless; they are honest followers of Tathagata and respect each other. He also witnesses that some senior monks are arrogant and dictators, who are engaged in competing with each other. Out of them, some consider themselves great and enlightened and others as dumb and foolish.

He is conscious of germs in internal politics of the monasteries. Nalanda's aim is to uplift human beings, but some learners slip and fall into dirt. Kumaril is not a part of any group. His studious and focused temperament is the cause of irritation and jealousy among some of his ilk. Such people show their resentment by calling him a bookworm behind his back, while some others find his simplicity as pretentious. They want to curse him but do not get the opportunity to do so.

But Kumaril, ignorant of all such matters, delves deep in the ocean of knowledge. His personality has transformed to become more intense and serious, increasing the envy and irritation of his adversaries.

He gets up in the wee hours, attends the morning prayers in front of the Buddha's statue, presents himself to his teacher after breakfast and participates in lectures and group discussions with his teachers. The discussionis today are on the topic, 'Comparative Study of Vedic and Buddhist Texts'.

Initiating the group discussion, the learned teacher states that the *Vedas* are inauthentic because they contain contradictory views, while the Buddhist texts are genuine by virtue of being based on realised truths of the Bodhisattva. Kumaril controls his urge to contradict the statement, but regretfully keeps quiet. The second speaker ridiculed the *Vedas* and calls them nonsensical while referring to Buddhist texts as the Ultimate Truth. This too provokes Kumaril, but he keeps quiet. The third speaker uses shallow words to describe the *Upanishads* as wild gossip, while the fourth criticises the Vedic texts as a flight of foolishness. This grieves Kumaril and a tear rolls down from the corners of his helpless eyes.

He wipes them away, but the ache in the heart melts like snow and tears flow out in a stream. His colleagues and teachers are bewildered to see this and wonder what pain is causing him so much hurt in the mind of this excellent and dedicated student! A teacher asks about it and Kumaril replies, "It is unbearable for me to hear even a single word of condemnation of the *Vedas*. I have been tolerating this baseless criticism for so many days, but today I could not control the hurt which flowed out of my eyes."

The very foundation of Buddhism was based on condemning the *Vedas*. The self-realised message of Gautam Buddha was not merely confined to the intellectual capacity of the Buddhist religious leaders whose *mantra* was simply condemnation and hatred. Kumaril's adversaries now find the opportunity to launch an attack on him. The most defiant among them asks Kumaril, "You, tell the truth and state your true identity. Are you not a devotee of the *Vedas* present here in disguise?"

Kumaril replies firmly in one sentence, "I am Kumaril!"

This utterance works as fuel for the fire. Kumaril's name is a dynamite which has been often discussed at Nalanda. He was guilty of Dharmakirti's untimely suicide and who could forgive him for that sin! Burning in the fire of vengeance, the Buddhist adversaries force him down from the roof of the highest attics but by the grace of God, he survives. Apart from some minor injury and damage to one eye, the rest of the body remains unhurt and he stands up immediately after falling down. He says, "The *Vedas* have protected me, so I will protect them throughout my life."

The supporters of Vedic religion start gathering around Kumaril as he is their hero. In the midst of the increasing debate, it is decided that in the presence of Vedic and Buddhist scholars, the one who gets defeated in the debate between Kumaril and his Buddhist teacher Dharmapal, would have to accept the religion of the conqueror or enter the fire. He defeats his Buddhist *guru*, Dharmapal, in a serious debate at Nalanda and then sets out on a campaign to restore Vedic religion across the country. A defeated Dharmapal enters the fire without converting his religion. The Magadh ruler appoints the victorious Kumaril as his chief priest and organises a huge Ashwamedha *yajna*. Many rulers from different parts of India participate in the *yajna* organised by the ruler of Magadh.

After the main worship, a grand banquet is held. The next day, the king of Magadh requests Guru Kumaril Bhatt to address the guests. In that grand ceremony witnessed by kings and royalty, Kumaril starts speaking...

"Respected Excellencies! Our Aranya culture, which grew

up under the umbrella of the *Vedas*, considers the whole earth as its family. Our ancient sages have taught us to respect all living beings, plants and Nature. The Vedic religion favours co-existence, respect, kindness, compassion and lofty values of life. Even the grandest of all buildings require continuous cleaning, painting and repairs. The same is the case with our ancient religion. The spider's web of vested interests had flourished in this grand palace. Along with fresh air from its open doors, dust and garbage also had entered. From time to time, various religious leaders and philosophers have cleaned the huge building in their respective eras with their intelligence and power of thought. Gautam Buddha did the same thing with his brilliance and divine personality, but unfortunately, his followers have, instead of cleaning the building, started demolishing it with their foolishness and over-enthusiasm. Today the challenge is to save our heritage from these lunatics. We have to do this work with both weapons and scriptures, else our civilisation will survive only in history.

"Excellencies, the nation which does not purify itself is oppressed by its enemies. Therefore, we have to rectify our faults ourselves.

"Today we are divided into innumerable religious sects. The mass movement to reform the Vedic religion, which was started by Gautam Buddha, has transformed itself into a new religion which has become a disease and against which it has received public support. The ideological enmity between the Hinayana and Mahayana is becoming fiercer day by day. If Siddhartha himself had seen this downfall, he would have felt hurt.

"Excellencies, division gives birth to a new division. Today there is a need to unite, not to divide, and the Vedic religion has the ability to maintain the geographical units of this vast land tied in one thread.

"The common layman is not expected to understand the deeper truths of life and live up to the level of sages blessed with ideological divinity. In such a situation, *Mimamsa*, that is, ritualistic practices can be a practical way of regularising and bringing uniformity in their life. Just as this horse-sacrifice is the grandest of the Vedic religious rites which has kept us connected, similarly social unification will be strengthened by following rituals in our daily life.

"Excellencies, while we need a vigorous intellectual movement to unite the masses, on the other hand, there is equally a need to take up arms to stop the conversions conducted through fraud or force. All of you should ponder on my point and take the necessary measures. Thank you!"

Saying this, Kumaril sitst down on his seat.

The auditorium unanimously bursts into applause at his statement and Vedic India begins to stand in the face of retaliation. The sun of Vedic religion is re-illumined the whole of North India, including Magadh and Gaudh with the glory of Kumaril's erudition. The victorious Kumaril now moves towards the south. As a result of his efforts, the Vedic *mantras* again start reverberating in the deserted delubrums.

The same national hero Kumaril had sacrificed himself today at the altar of his ideals.

□

30

Meeting Mandan

Acharya Kumaril had said to Shankar at the time of self-sacrifice, "O greatest Shankar, if you want to illumine the Vedanta path, win over the glorious Mandan Mishra, the best among the scholars and as famous as any ruler. He is famous for preaching the path of *karma* and is known as Vishwaroop. He is ready, diligent and a great householder in the Vedic path. You go to him in the city of Mahishmati where Vishwaroop is my best representative. Persuade his wife to become your follower by making him a witness and winning her in debate."

Shankar resolves to go to Mahismati and meet Mandan Mishra. Mahishmati was the capital of the very majestic Emperor Kartavirya, popularly known as Sahastrabahu. Emperor Kartavirya was unparalleled in sacrifice, charity, penance, *yoga*, *shruti*, strength and victory. He had taken Ravana as a captive, who had set out for world conquest. In order to rescue him, Sage Pulsatya himself had to come. Due to conflict with Maharishi Jamadagni, he was consumed by Lord Parshuram's anger. After a long journey, Shankar's mind is delighted to see the splendid beauty of Mahishmati on the banks of the holy River Narmada and he camps in a garden on its banks.

Shankar rests in the garden, performs his daily rituals in the morning and as the sun rises, he goes out to locate the address and home of Mandan Mishra. The women who gathr at the riverbank to fetch water, bow their heads to this sage and receive his blessings. When Shankar asks the address of Mandan Mishra's house, an ever-pleasing, eloquent woman replies, "Lord, from here, this road leads straight to Panditji's house. Even animals and birds in his house talk in Sanskrit. The house outside which the parrot and *myna* have a serious conversation in Sanskrit in the cage is the house of Mandan Mishra."

The Acharya and his band of disciples proceed along the path with a smile.

After walking a little further, they notice a row of grand buildings of the elite class. The beautiful buildings, their huge gates, windows, decorations are eye-catching. Somewhere beautiful chariots stand and at some gates, well-built horses stand neighing. Seeing this spectacle, an awestruck Acharya keeps on moving forward. The heat of the sun has started increasing but the destination is yet not visible. At a little distance is heard the beautiful voice of a *myna,* who ss talking to a parrot in her melodious voice in Sanskrit language.

The pilgrims are thrilled to have reached their destination. What a house it is of Mandan Mishra! It is a high-platformed magnificent palace. The disciples reach the grand gate by climbing the stairs higher than the path but are politely stopped outside by the gatekeepers.

Today is the observance of *mahashradha*. The royal priest Mandan Mishra is preoccupied, hence visitors are not allowed. When the disciples convey this scene to their *guru*, he climbs up the stairs and reaches the main gate. Seeing his enlightened aura, the gatekeepers do not have the courage to stop him and by the time they realise their duty, the Acharya enters the building with ease. After crossing the gallery, Shankar notices a good-looking man with two sages in the delubrum built in the huge courtyard. He assumes that the good-looking man has to be Mandan Mishra! On the other hand, the ritualistic leader, Mandan Mishra is irritated to see his uninvited guest, an unknown monk, at the *shradha* ritual is unacceptable because traditionally the arrival of a monk is prohibited at such an event.

Outraged at this interference, Mandan Mishra asks with contempt, "Hey you with the tonsured head, what are you doing here? Why did you come without an invitation? Are you drunk or have lost your balance of mind due to some contaminated food you may have consumed as to illegally enter my house?"

A calm and peaceful Shankar resolutely reminds Mandan of his *guru* Kumaril and narrates the details of his last conversation. Mandan immediately realises his mistake and invites Shankar to partake food with him. But Shankar had not arrived to eat food. He says in a solemn voice, "O gentleman, I have not come to you to beg for food; I have come to engage with you in a debate."

Mandan Mishra replies with a happy heart, "O great sage, today I should complete this ritual. From tomorrow onwards I will fulfil your wish as per the law."

Acharya Shankar accepts this offer and returns home.

□

31

Debate Episode

Next day, when Acharya Shankar reaches Mandan Mishra's residence at the appointed time, the scene has changed. The gatekeepers escort him inside with respect and everyone stares at him with amazement in the huge meeting hall filled with scholars, priests and intellectuals of all hues. Everyone is certain initially itself that this young contestant would lose his aura to Pandit Mandan Mishra. Their faith is not misplaced as they had seen many warriors, sages, philosophers come to this intellectual arena and return humbled in defeat. Even today they had come to enjoy and return with the same feeling of thrill.

This had become almost a regular source of intellectual entertainment for the people of Mahishmati, so a crowd of onlookers and spectators fill not only the hall but even the corridors outside the hall.

As soon as Shankar reaches the meeting hall, the priest makes him sit on the appointed seat. His disciples are made to sit behind him. On the opposite side of Shankar sits Mandan Mishra. The proceedings start with an invocation by the priests.

The solemn voice of the scholar who is conducting the programme announces, "Esteemed guests, today the debate between Acharya Shankar and Pandit Mandan Mishra will begin in this house, but before that, Acharya Shankar will present his proposal according to the accepted tradition. Subsequently, Pandit Mandan Mishra, in case of any disagreement, can exercise the right to rebutt. A scholar shall be nominated to act as the mediator with the consent of both the parties. Further rules of the debate will be in the hands of the mediator under whose guidance, both sides will take their oath and open the debate." Pausing for a moment, he requests Acharya Shankar to present the subject of the debate in the house.

The audience, out of curiosity, looks at Shankar standing silently with a glowing countenance and well-built body. He begins to speak in an eloquent voice which starts reverberating in the large hall, "Excellencies, the glory of Vedanta is supernatural, so its promotion is the goal of my life. Vedanta is as cool as the moon and removes all pain and anguish in the world, but, Pandit Mandan Mishra has disregarded the Vedanta by taking shelter on the path of *karma*. That is why dear Mandan, you should accept the best path propagated by me or else be prepared to have a debate with me."

Filled with self-confidence, Mandan Mishra stands erect in his place and says boldly, "Even if the thousand-headed cobra (*sheshnaag)* comes before me as a defendant, even then I will never accept your imaginary philosophy except the *Shruti*-accepted *karma* rituals. To refute your views, I am ready to debate." Mandan Mishra raises his right arm and roars, "I, Mandan Mishra can counter even Yamraj, the destroyer of life. Vedanta considers God to be the giver of the fruit of action, but I can prove that the giver of the fruit is *karma* itself. There is no need for God. So, you can contradict me."

Knowing that the debate is certain to be prolonged, the crowd is convinced that the clash will be fierce. Both sides are determined to debate; now it is the time to nominate a mediator. The audience listens in amazement to the voice of Acharya Shankar, "I propose that the piquant-voiced Ubhaya Bharati, the wise wife of Pandit Mandan Mishra, should be the judge of our debate."

Mandan Mishra is baffled at this proposal, but has no objection to it, so he agrees. The wise Ubhaya gracefully accepts the important responsibility assigned in the midst of the sound of applause. By making this suggestion, Acharya Shankar wins the heart of the public even before the debate has begun. The scholar Ubhaya, sitting on the seat of the mediator, invites Acharya Shankar to take the oath in her melodious voice.

The Acharya takes the oath, "According to the principle of my monistic Vedanta path, the *jiva* and Brahm are one; there is no duality in them. There is evidence of this in the *Upanishad* too. Oh Mandan, if I get defeated in this debate, I will give up my saffron clothes and take to wearing white garments."

In response, Mandan Mishra replies, "I consider the *karmic* part of the *Vedas* to be proof. I do not consider the *Upanishads* as proof; *karma* is prime. Being an interpreter, it is my promise that if I am defeated in this debate, I will leave the family life and renunciate."

The learned Ubhaya, seated on the judge's seat, places fragrant garlands of fresh flowers around the necks of the two knowledgeable philosophers sitting opposite each other in the hall and announces, "Whosever's garland withers first during the debate will be considered the loser."

Now begins the debate – on one side is Acharya Shankar, anxious to hoist the flag of monotheism, while on the other is Mandan Mishra, the commander of Dvaita and *Mimamsa*. The hall is held spellbound by the duel between logic with logic, *shruti* with *shruti*, *mantra* with *mantra*, intellect with intellect, memory with memory.

It all gets over. The tri-marked Acharya Shankar, with his easeful smile, says to Mandan Mishra, "Monism as ultimate knowledge is the only goal of the *Vedas*."

Prompt comes Mandan Mishra reply, "*Karma* (action) is the meaning of the *Vedas*. Liberation is attained as a result of action and without action, liberation is not possible." Mandan further adds, "O Brahmin priest, you people consider *jiva* and Brahm to be the same, but is there any positive proof of this?"

Responding, Shankar says, "O best scholar, evidence of this is abundant in the *Upanishads*. Sages like Uddalaka have responded to the disciple Shwetketu in the words, *'Tattva masi Shvetaketo'* (O Shwetketu, you are a form of Brahma). This is the biggest proof."

Mandan Mishra disagrees and argues, "Just as words like *hum phat*, etc. are meaningless but by chanting them only removes sin, similarly *tattva masi's* purpose is only in chanting and self-study."

The Acharya counter-argues, "*Hum phat* does not reveal any meaning, but the meaning of *tattva masi* is self-evident, then how can it be accepted only for incantation?"

Mandan says, "O superior Brahmin, *tattva masi* does not reveal the unity of the living entity and the Divine; in fact, it praises the performer of the sacrificial sequences and so it is a part of the process."

Acharya refutes him, "How can *tattva masi* and *aham Brahmasmi*, etc. be integral to knowledge? How can they be a part of performative law?"

How could Mandan believe this! He says, "O sage, the true meaning of *tattva masi* is that one should see the Supreme in the being. This being never disturbs the unity of Supreme." Mandan further adds, "Sir, Vedanta accepts this sentence as a representation of unity, but in the opinion of interpretative analysis (*Mimamsa)*, this sentence counteracts the concordance of soul and Supreme."

Shankar strongly counters this statement of Mandan Mishra. The latter is no less than Shankar and demolishes the latter's arguments from the root.

Acharya Shankar counters Mandan Mishra's arguments by citing examples from *Vedas, Shastras* and *Upanishads.*

The audience is captivated by the arguments of one and surprised by the light of the intellect of the other. Seeing no end to the debate, Ubhaya, who is seated on the judgement seat, says in her humble voice, "You continue the debate; I would like to attend to the arrangements for food."

As soon as she gets up and leaves, the debate proceeds again. As much as Shankar refutes monism, Mandan Mishra with his brilliant talent counters him the very next moment. As a result, *Shruti, Vedas, Puranas* and *Agama Nigams* serve at times like shields and at times like swords. The amphitheatre echoes with shrieks and shrills, with sighs and wows, but the spirit of the warriors refuses to wane. Then Ubhaya arrives again in the hall and requests her husband and Acharya Shankar to take food and alms.

On her request, the debate is adjourned for lunch-break. In the mess, Mandan Mishra takes food while Acharya takes alms. The audience too takes advantage of the lunch-break.

After the lunch-break, the debate starts again in the meeting hall. Both the warriors struggle with arguments and facts till sunset. At sunset, this intellectual exercise is postponed for the next day.

Religious debate has been an intellectual festival in the Vedic tradition of India. In this wonderful culture of ideological freedom, both folk-education and folk-rituals existed together. Through debates, outdated ideas were refuted by debaters and the winds of new ideas were welcomed, infusing freshness and novelty in the minds of the society. Here the common man could simultaneously enjoy both entertainment and intellectual development. The younger generation got to learn the art to express their thoughts in a decent and courteous manner.

There was a difference of opinion during the debate, but there were no differences in the hearts. Respect for each other and attentive hearing to each other's views was the first condition of the debate. In the debate, the Vedic tradition was carried on beautifully. Both sides could disagree with each other and cut short the other's arguments, but there was no sense of malignancy or animosity. The whole process seemed like the churning of an ocean of knowledge for the audience which knew that this was not a battle between gods and demons; it was but a search for truth by both sides.

Here in the hall, the precious gem-like thoughts that emanated from the churning of the ocean of knowledge, dazzled the listeners by their brilliance. How such seventeen days passed in exchange of knowledge, no one knew. People would enter the meeting hall soon after sunrise and Ubhaya would sit on the judge's seat. Pandit Mandan Mishra and Acharya Shankar would be seated on their rugs. Fresh flower garlands would adorn their necks and the debate would begin. During the lunch-break, Ubhaya, as was her wont, would regularly invite her husband for food and Acharya for alms. This intellectual battle would end very day with sunset.

□

32

Debate Episode

Today is the eighteenth day, but neither the audience nor the competitors are satiated. No aspect of the ancient *Samhitas* has not been touched upon in these seventeen days! Kapil, Vashishta, Yagyavalka, Gargi, Manu, Parshuram, Vishwamitra, Janmadagani, Bhrigu, etc. are among the sages whose names were raised by these speakers in their arguments but the decisive moment is yet to come.

Today again the debate is scheduled to begin at the appointed time. A large gathering of religious scholars, philosophers, religion lovers and devotees from all over the country are gathered and there is no vacant place left. Mandan Mishra sits happily, glowing with confidence, on his seat. On the other hand, Acharya Shankar with a *tri* mark on his forehead is seen filled with pious ecstasy while the audience eagerly awaits to receive the intellectual dose for the day.

The seat of the judge is also vacant. The learned Ubhaya Bharati hasn't yet arrived. There is a period of restrained laughter and happiness in the hall. People are busy greeting each other. Soon Ubhaya arrives and occupies her seat with dignity. Sitting on her judgement seat, she gestures and two garlands made of freshly blooming fragrant flowers are placed before her. She makes the two contestors wear the garlands and signals for the debate to begin. Acharya Shankar again initiates the debate. When he starts speaking in his calm voice, as usual, silence descends on the hall with no other sound is heard except for his voice.

He says, "O great scholar, it is written in the *Mundaka Upanishad* that the learned Brahmins of the *Vedas*, on seeing the fruits obtained by action, moved towards renunciation because salvation is not attained by any action. The fruits of *karma* decay. Just as death is certain after birth, so also after union, separation is certain. If salvation is achieved through action, its destruction would have been certain. *Moksha* is the form of the soul, which is available at all times.

"The *Kathopanishad* also believes that when the veil of ignorance is removed, the soul shines like the sun. This evidence seems to weaken the role of action but in the entire *Vedas*, there is no evidence to prove the weakness of knowledge." Saying this, he pauses. The audience listens to him with awe. When this argument gets over, everyone turns to look at Mandan Mishra. There are clear signs of perplexity on his face. He does not present any argument and looks as if he is entangled in himself. He is lost in a deep whirlpool of thoughts. He feels as of his memory has betrayed him and his mind is completely blank. His body temperature soars and the audience notices that he is sweating and the garland of flowers around his neck is withering slowly.

The tension is visible not only on Mandan Mishra's face, but also in his body posture. He looks dejected in front of Shankar's irrefutable reasoning. He tries to restrain himself, but he observes his defeat vissible on the faces of the masses. The learned Ubhaya, sitting on the judge's seat, discharges her duty by approving the arguments presented by Shankar. She says, "Both of you should go to receive alms."

The audience is full of praise at the prudence and wise judgement of learned Ubhaya. Mandan Mishra has by now recovered from his defeat and bowing to his future *guru*, Acharya Shankar, he requests, "Acharya, I have to renunciate and give up the householder's life according to my oath. Kindly initiate me on this path."

By the time Acharya Shankar could complete his arguments,

Ubhaya renounces the judgement seat and assuming the role of a wife, says, "O Acharya, in the scriptures, the wife is said to be the better half part of the husband, that is, *ardhangini,* so without defeating me, your victory is only half, not complete. Therefore, before making my husband your disciple, you should participate in a debate with me. If you defeat me, then only can you treat my husband as your disciple."

□

33

Shankar-Ubhaya Debate

Acharya Shankar gently looks at the face of the wise Ubhaya. He had not expected this sudden challenge. Between him and his complete victory now stands Ubhaya as a wall. After all, her existence is at stake. She was shocked at the defeat of her learned and proud husband. Today the royal priest of Mahishmati, the legend of *Mimamsa*, Mandan Mishra stands defeated. Under such circumstances, how could his wife remain a mute spectator? She has studied all the four *Vedas* with interest. She had acquired knowledge of all the religious scriptures, philosophy, grammar, verses, *Upanishads* in her parental home. Apart from being skilled in household duties, she was efficient in logic ad philosophy. For preserving the reputation and safety of her husband, like Savitri she had the strength to fight the God of Death and was prepared to debate with Acharya Shankar.

Hearing her desire for debate, Acharya Shankar hesitates for a moment and then replies, "O Goddess, it is not proper for me to argue with you because decency does not permit me to do so. I request you to please drop this thought."

The scholar Ubhaya challenges him instead, "Sir, why do you consider a woman weak? The debate between great Saint Yajnavalkya and learned Gargi in the past is unforgettable. King Janaka also debated with Sulabha; even then his fame did not decrease. So accept my request and debate with me. In case you refuse to debate with me, then it would tantamount to accepting your defeat."

Now Acharya has no option but to debate. He also is aware that the sympathy of the entire house is with the defeated side. He ponders for a moment and knows that none of his work is motivated by personal attachment or aversion. He is well aware of the inaccessibility of the path that he has chosen to pledge for the preservation of the ancient cultural tradition of India. The victory in the debate would not be achieved for the satisfaction of his ego; it wouold be instead a small oblation in the great *yajna* performed for national integration. This *yajna* could not be disrupted. It needed continuous oblation for which the next offering was being presented by the learned Ubhaya herself.

Acharya offers his consent. The debate is resumed after the lunch-break. Learned Ubhaya's extensive talent begins to manifest itself in her sharp questions and concrete answers. From the very beginning itself, she appears to be discussing one topic after another like a torrential river flowing from the mountains. The house feels that the Vedanta's boat will not last long in this fierce onslaught, but Acharya Shankar, with the stoic calm of the Himalayas, wraps the Ganga of her knowledge in the locks of Vedanta philosophy, just like Lord Shiva Himself. This knowledge-*yajna* continues for the next seventeen days.

The initial fire raging in the mind of the scholarly Ubhaya begins to wane to become a thin summer stream and it now appears that her defeat is not far away. On the eighteenth day; she tactfully changes the mode of her questions and reverses everything. So far, she had strongly countered Acharya's arguments on the Supreme Soul, *Vedanta* and *Upanishad*, but now she hs realised that the Acharya's field of learning acquired at a very young age is so vast that it cannot be overcome.

□

34

Knowledge of *Kamasutra* Worked

It was realised by Mandan's wife that it was not possible to win over the Acharya in the contemplation of scriptures and it also meant that her defeat was certain. Her marital life, prestige, splendour as the wife of the royal priest, social status – all were at stake, because with the victory of Acharya, Mandan had to renunciate as a result of which everything that she possessed was going to be washed away in the flood of this impending disaster.

For her it was an existential crisis. She had to defeat the Acharya in order to protect her self-esteem. She thought that since Acharya Shankar had renunciated during childhood itself, so he would be deprived of the knowledge of *Kamasutra*. She said to herself, 'I will win him through this treatise.' So she opened the attack, "How many are the arts of *kama*? What is their forms? Where do they reside? Where is their position in the dark fortnight? How do these arts reside in a woman and in a man?"

Her questions leaves the house baffled and Acharya Shankar too feels at a loss for the reply. He however comes up with a very smart thought because he knows, 'if I do not say anything, I will be defeated and if I reply, then the dignity of a monk will be violated.' So he very politely replies, "*Devi*, if you ask classical questions, I will be able to answer them; asking a monk about *kama* is not decent."

But the learned Ubhaya is not the one to give up. She immediately asks, "Why sir, is *Kamasutra* not a scripture? Monks can overcome their senses and remain unaffected even in the discussion of *Kamasutra*."

On hearing this, even Mandan Mishra, who is watching silently, is unable to intervene, "Such a conversation with a monk is not appropriate."

The scholarly Ubhaya replies in a stern voice, "The knowledgeable have conquered the vices of lust, anger, greed, etc. If their mind is disturbed even on analysis of the *Kamasutra*, then their knowledge becomes incomplete and immature. In such a situation, can he be called your *guru*?"

No answer comes to Mandan Mishra's mind, but Acharya Shankar realises the wit of scholar Ubhaya and says, "Mother, to answer your questions, I will have to do study of this field. Give me one month for this and I will gain experience by entering someone else's body and answer your questions in writing."

Ubhaya asks, "O great monk, will not your renunciation get affected if you were to enter someone else's body?"

Acharya Shankar replies with a question, "Madam, what does it matter if a person born in a Brahmin family in this birth was an outcaste in the previous birth?"

On receiving this reply, Ubhaya is completely outwitted.

□

35

Entering another Body

Acharya is now worried as to how the study of the art of *kama* can be accomplished within the time limit of one month? He and the other monks are now going in the eastern direction. After many days of ravel, they reach a beautiful but isolated forest. They hope to reach some township after crossing this forest. Suddenly they are confronted by a crowd of royal courtiers. The tone of their collective lament disturbs the peace of the forest.

On reaching them, it is found that King Amaruk had come to hunt in the forest where his heartbeats suddenly stopped and he died. That's why his queens, children and courtiers are weeping in grief.

Acharya Shankar promptly decides to enter the dead body of the king through the power of yoga. He, along with his disciples, climb a high and inaccessible hill where they find a cave on the banks of a lake containing sweet water. He says, "I will leave this body by the force of *yoga* and enter the body of the king while you guys stay here amidst the fruit trees and sweet water. I will return to my body again before one month."

The disciples notice that Acharya has sat down in the lotus position and is engrossed in meditation. For some time, he appears to be in meditation but within a few moments, his body becomes lifeless and still, before collapsing. The disciples respectfully carry him to a safe place in the cave.

From the top of this hill, the disciples notice the king's lifeless body coming to life and breathe again. His heart has begun to beat again. It seems unbelievable, but it is true. The people around him stop wailing and begin to dance with happiness. They notice the king open his eyes, rise up and sit down as if he had just woken up from a deep slumber. His companions, relatives and wives stand transfixed while his servants escort them all on horses and palanquins towards the capital.

In the midst of the loud cheers, King Amaruk reaches the palace. He delivers judgements in the court, meets foreign envoys, takes decisions regarding the affairs of ministers, scholars and delivers harsh punishment to the wicked.

Such diligence is manifested in him for the first time. Now he is seen to be taking greater interest in public welfare than in hunting and fighting battles. Within six-seven days, there is a change in the working of the kingdom. For the first time, the guilty ones receive harsh punishment and the righteous are able to live their life with dignity. The effect of good governance is now apparent. The merchants enthusiastically engage in business, while the farmers start working diligently in agricultural activities. Teachers start emphasising the importance of education in *gurukuls* and Nature showers its mercy. The heavy rains do not cause any problems and the rivers get filled with water and gardens bloom with fruits and flowers.

The king returns from court to attend to his queens instead of getting drunk and intoxicated. His ministers, courtiers, doctors, moneylenders, army, subjects, royal family are happy and amazed at the king's transformation all of a sudden. The king now devotes time to reading and discussions with learned priests. He studies excellent books, apart from the *Kamasutra* of Maharishi Vatsyayan. People too are happy on hearing the news of their king spending his time in the royal library every day besides taking up the writing of a book.

The sudden change in the personality of their ruler arouses suspicion in the minds of the priests. The head priest thinks that possibly some divine soul has entered the king's body as he had now begun to use his ability, talent and power for the welfare of his subjects. The head priest orders that all adjoining forests and caves should be searched to find if any dead body lay somewhere. If so, then it should be burned promptly, so that the divine spirit is unable to return and the king's subjects can enjoy the benefits of devotion and good governance continuously.

But there is a slight delay in this decision. By the time the king's men can reach the cave on top of the mountain, Acharya returns to his original body after acquiring theoretical and practical knowledge about the *Kamasutra.* Meanwhile the Acharya and his beloved disciples descend from the top of the mountain and embark on their path to Mahishmati.

In the royal palace, the king's heart stops beating and he dies, surrounded by his family and well-wishers.

□

36

Revisiting Mahishmati

In Mahishmati, the news of Acharya Shankar's return spreads like wild fire. Crowds of people arrive to visit the guest at Mandan Mishra's house. Acharya replies to all the questions put forth by Ubhaya in writing after reading and at which she accepts her defeat with dignity.

Acharya initiates Mandan Mishra into renunciation and gives him a new name, 'Sureshvara'. His virtuous wife is also honoured by the disciples at the behest of Acharya. Mahishmati gives a heartfelt farewell to its genius royal priest, Mandan Mishra and his learned wife Ubhaya while hailing Acharya Shankar for his intelligence. The Mishra couple, in turn, dedicate their entire property to the Acharya for the purpose of learning philosophy before they renounce.

Acharya has been a non-possessor. He constitutes a committee of distinguished citizens of Mahishmati to hand over a Sanskrit school to them and the responsibility of opening a food corner for the devotees who circumambulate the Narmada river.

The new ascetic, Mandan Mishra is given the knowledge of *Tattvopdesh* in the form of *guru's* grace. The news of Acharya Shankar's victory over the great interpreter Pandit Mandan Mishra and the initiation of husband and wife into the ascetic religion is broadcast everywhere. Wherever the story reaches, people begin to discuss, highly with interest, the knowledge, courage, victory and personality of this wonderful monk.

Now the aura of Acharya Shankar's fame starts spreading far and wide.

□

37

Victory on Kapalikas

The debate with Mandan Mishra and learned Ubhaya imparts additional faith and vigour to Acharya Shankar. His influence begins to spread beyond the boundaries of not only the cities and villages, but also the states. He declares, "Those who do not have faith in the *Vedas* and those who do not believe in monism are cordially invited to debate or else they must declare their faith in monism and in the *Vedas*."

His announcement causes a stir all around. The first and fastest reaction comes from the Kapalikas, who have established their dominance over the Srisailam shrine. The style of worship of the Kapalikas is very different. They are the worshippers of Mahabhairav, an incarnation of Lord Shiva. Alcohol, human sacrifice and animal sacrifice are essential in their rituals. They do not accept faith in anyone other than Kaal Bhairav and challenge anyone who wants to debate.

Acharya accepts their invitation and begins his journey to Srisailam with his disciples. He would wake up early in the morning in the wee hours, start his journey after taking a break from daily activities and worship. When the afternoon sun gets more intense, his group of monks dressed in ochre robes take shelter in the shade of trees. They continue their travel after food and rest. They spend the night at a place where they can reach before sunset.

The residents of the villages falling on their way see Shankar, make arrangements for welcoming hiim and receive the benefit of religious knowledge from him. Acharya Shankar's attractive personality and melodious speech mesmerise the people. In a simple and interesting manner he makes people understand monism of Vedantic philosophy. Enchanted listeners become his disciples in every village, although they follow other faiths.Their doubts are resolved by Shankar. His speech inspires people to unite in one thread, irrespective of the differences in opinions. He marches forward, eradicating regional prejudices and explains the importance of diversity of India.

His disciples follow their *guru* in ethics. His entire journey is like a virtuous river, which moves forward, nourishing the land, vegetation, stones, sand and animals falling in its path. This journey, which started from Mahishmati, now breaks at Panchavati in Maharashtra. After the reception, Acharya wants to visit the holy place with his disciples, where Lord Ram lived with wife Sita and brother Lakshman. He finds that the ancient Ram temple is mismanaged and broken. Instead of the sounds of prayers and chants, the place echoes with the chatter of bats and crickets. Seeing the plight and filth of the temple, Acharya takes up a broom to clean the dirt and this embarrasses the villagers. They clean the entire courtyard and burn the garbage. The bats also fly away due to the smoke. The people fetch water to wash and sanctify the temple.

Acharya anoints the temple with *Veda mantras*. Mandan Mishra, who has now become Sureshvaracharya, performs the worship rituals in the temple. The local villagers are assigned the responsibility of running this newly renovated temple. The Brahmins of the village promise to conduct regular prayers. That night the place looks like a religious fair. The entire night, hymns are sung. The faith of the people is able to re-establish the temple just in one night. The very next day, the villagers begin the construction of a monastery near the temple.

The group of young monks sweep out the spider webs of indolence formed in the minds of the society, clear the dust of illusions, cut the shackles of mental distances so that a new consciousness, a new enthusiasm and a new faith may emerge in the society. Wherever these pilgrims move in a procession, they wipe clean the dry bushes of despair and animosity.

After spending a few days in the idyllic atmosphere of Panchavati, this group of monks reaches Pandarpur, located on the banks of River Chandrabhaga. On seeing Shankar, the people begin to believe that Lord Vishnu himself has appeared as Shankar at Pandarpur on the request of the devotee Pundarik. The belief runs so deep that this place becomes an important and vibrant pilgrimage centre.

Devotees from distant places of Maharashtra come here to visit Lord Vitthal and Rukmani. Here also Acharya is warmly welcomed. He narrates interesting stories of the *Upanishads* to the devotees, besides presenting discourses on the esoteric topics of monism in a simple manner. On seeing the Acharya and his group of monks, the residents of Pandarpur and the pilgrims feel as if Vitthal himself has incarnated. He is surrounded by devotees for as many days as he stays there.

Here, one day, Acharya sings a hymn in his melodious voice in praise of Lord Vitthal. It arouses emotional feelings in the devotees and becomes famous as *pulkit stotra.*

Moving towards Srisailam, Acharya Shankar and his disciples visit all the religious places on their way, staying where required, camping here and there and enlightening the local residents on the value of labour and knowledge donation. He moves ahead, providing cooperation for purification, repair and re-construction of religious places.

Information on their activities reaches the ears of Karakacha, the king of Srisailam. The city's most able debaters are given the responsibility to refute the Vedanta philosophy of Shankar. However, the city eagerly awaits the arrival of Acharya Shankar. The Kapalikas are eager to confront him. Located on the banks of holy River Tungabhadra is one of the nine *jyotirlingas* of the country. It is revered and worshipped as the ancient city of pilgrimage.

Acharya Shankar visits and worships this divine *jyotirlinga*. According to the accepted tradition, he has to first argue with the Kapalikas. All their preparations however go in vain. Shankar is unable to get his turn to debate because Sureshvaracharya and Padmapada had already defeated the Kapalikas. Kapalikas' reputation is at stake. The defeat agitates the Kapalikas. Krakacha, the king of Kapalikas, gives Ugra Bhairav the responsibility to kill Acharya deceitfully.

The logical and well-built disciple group acts as the armour of Acharya against which only deceit can kill him. Ugra Bhairav, in disguise, joins the circle of disciples around Shankar. The pure-hearted and caring Acharya Shankar is glad to see the humility and tireless service of Ugra Bhairav, his new disciple, who faithfully stands nearby, day and night in his service. He is always first in worship and last of all to eat and sleep also. He would do every task with enthusiasm. Acharya Shankar, pleased at his service, says to him one day in solitude, "I am happy with your service; whenever you need anything, ask for it. Do not hesitate."

The hypocritical disciple, who, like Ravana, had become a sage in the guise of a monk, keeps thinking day and night about the method to adopt to kill the Acharya. He says humbly with folded hands at his feet, "O *guru*, you are famous for omniscience and kindness in the world. You are in this body only for charity. The seeker who comes to your shelter never goes empty-handed."

Hearing this, Acharya Shankar smiles softly and says, "O disciple, I have told you, feel free to ask for whatever you want. Whatever belongs to me, belongs to my disciples."

Knowing that the iron is hot, Kapalika says, "O Lord, I have taken a vow to please Lord Bhairav. He has asked me to offer the head of a king or omniscient in my dream. I have been unable to do so for a long time. I am troubled. If you give me your head for this noble cause, Lord Bhairav will be pleased and you will get salvation." Taking a moment's breath, the Kapalika continues, "O great sage, by giving your head, you will acquire wonderful fame in the world like Dadhichi and my deed will be accomplished. Decide soon." Saying this, the cunning person prostrates at the feet of Acharya Shankar.

Acharya Shankar bends forward and lifts Kapalika kindly and says lovingly, "This body will definitely be destroyed one day even if it is protected with effort. It would be a matter of happiness if this mortal body is of any use to anyone." He further adds, "Look, when I am alone, then you come to me. I will give you my head. My students are not with me at that time, neither is any other person, so at that time you can fulfil your desire." He then tells him the time and place of his solitary *samadhi.* A surprised Kapalika goes away, happy at obtaining the fruit of his obeisances.

At the appointed time the next day, in his original form and with a *tripunda* on his forehead, carrying a trident, a sword and wearing a garland of bones around his neck, reeking of alcohol, Kapalika reaches the designated spot where Acharya Shankar is meditating in isolation. At that time, there is no one except Acharya because most of the disciples had gone to bathe.

To fulfil the wish of Kapalika, Acharya sits on the *siddhasana* and concentrates to get absorbed in meditation. Kapalika takes up the sword to fulfil his desire and moves towards Acharya to behead him. He rushes towards him as his wish is about to be fulfilled in a few moments. Reaching near the Acharya, he raises his sword to strike. Suddenly someone hits him sharply from behind and he falls to the ground with his sword. When he tries to get up, he finds that someone's sharp sword had cut off the hand from which he hd been going to chop the head of Acharya Shankar.

A strong fountain of blood spurts out from his severed hand and the sharp sword of the attacker chops off his limbs like vegetables. He has wounds on his back, abdomen, legs, waist, neck; everywhere. Far from attacking first, it is not even possible to save himself. He dies in his own pool of blood.

In fact, Sanandan was keeping an eye on Kapalika and as soon as his spy informed him about Kapalika's arrival with weapons, Sanandan hid in *guru's* secluded cave and attacked Kapalika, even before he could attack the *guru* and thus sent him to hell.

The untouched Acharya is still in *samadhi*. Kapalika's deathly groan breaks his concentration. He hears frantic groans emerging from blood-splattered Sanandan and like Narasimha understands the sequence of events. Sanandan bows to *guruji* and entreats him to stay alert against the wicked. The body of the furious Bhairav is removed from the place. All the disciples appreciate Sanandan's courage and fortitude in saving their *guru's* life from Ugra Bhairav, the sinner's, hands.

□

38
Victory March

The news of the tragic end of Ugra Bhairav spreads like wildfire in Srisailam. Seeing his mighty body in pieces, fear spreads among the Kapalikas. All kinds of true and false stories begin to spread among the common people. Stories about Acharya's divinity, miraculous powers and consent to forsake his life even for the sake of the others are on people's tongues. The peace-loving common man breathes a sigh of relief at the death of Ugra Bhairav.

Not only does the reign of terror spread by Ugra Bhairav come to an end, even his dominance is nowhere to be seen. Influenced by Acharya and his group of disciples, many Kapalikas get attracted towards the teachings of monism.

After enlightening the people of Srisailam with the Vedantic flavour, Acharya and his disciples take the path of Gokarna. Acharya Shankar walks in the forefront with Sanandan and Sureshvarananda following one step behind and behind them come the rest of the other disciples. All of them move at a brisk pace, followed by dedicated people. After them follow the bullock carts carrying the goods of their daily use.

Acharya walks fast and the others have to run to keep apace with him. Ever since the glory of Acharya has increased, it has become difficult to move through the village. Villagers receive prior information about Acharya's route and erect welcome arches made with banana stems and leaves on the borders of ther village. They stand with folded hands in reverence, carrying fruits, sweets, food and drinking water. The fresh mango leaves swing in the wind as festoons.

Acharya halts to accept the welcome from the women performing the ritual of lighting a lamp on the plate of worship. The crowd garlands him with strings of flowers while some apply the vermillion mark on his forehead; still others offer full grains from a distance. Those who do not want to penetrate the throng feel satisfied at saluting him from far.

After the ritualistic reception, Acharya stands on a high platform to address the people, who are pushing against each other to catch a proper glimpse of him and hear his blissful voice. There is a clamour, a hustle and bustle, but as soon as his voice resonates, pindrop silence ensues. Each becomes silent and the only voice to be heard is that of the Acharya, who says, "Excellencies of the land of excellence, you are the children of great warriors. Your ancestors have created a great nation on earth with their knowledge, penance and virility. They were well equipped with both scriptures and weapons.

"Our ancestors include not only the great sages and kings but also the talented craftsmen, wonderful scientists, inventors, astronomers, architectural experts, city planners and accomplished businessmen. We had made progress in the physical and the divine and in all dimensions of life, but as is the order of Nature, we could not maintain our qualities over time. The petty personal interests became prominent and the whole society began to divide into factions and sects.

"The *varna* system for centuries made the nation prosperous by promoting division of work and genetic skill, with every person getting the opportunity to choose the profession and field of interest and develop his skill but here birth was given primacy. There entered a perversion of who is high and who is low, which eventually turned into untouchability. When it was retaliated against by the low, it was repressed by the high. The wheel of progress of the nation has come to a halt due to this mutual struggle.

"O children of nectar, remember your strength and take out the nation's chariot with collective effort from the morass it is bogged down in. The soul and the Supreme Soul are one. Just as salt is present in every drop of the ocean, in the same manner the God that resides in me resides in you all. Thus, to hate each other is an insult to the Almighty.

"O best people, it is said in our *Vedas* and *Upanishads* that there is only one truth. Scholars may refer to it in many ways, but it is only one. In the same way, all religions, all sects, ultimately worship only one God; so the enmity between sects is futile.

"O best devotees, just as there is no quarrel between Lord Vishnu and Lord Shiva, similarly there is no dispute between Lord Ganesha and Goddess Shakti. Consider all as the various *avatars* or forms of God and worship that indestructible one."

Suddenly a ruckus breaks out in the crowd as a defiant person stands up and shouts, "We do not agree with you. I am the follower of faith. We are worshippers of Maha Bhairav and our method of worship is different from that of Vaishnavas. Our banquet is different, worship is different, deities are different and offerings are also different. Our mark on the forehead is different, dress is also different. How can we live with the hypocritical Vaishnavas and worshippers of female goddesses? They have to either accept our true faith by abandoning their condemnable beliefs or fight against us. No one should think that we are dead due to the death of Kal Bhairav. The flame of vengeance burns in our hearts and we will not yield to your false propaganda."

Acharya replies in a solemn voice, "If any faith considers itself to be superior, then there is no trouble. The problem arises when it considers only itself to be superior and the others as inferior. It is then that enmity grows. God is one; just as your friends call you by one name, your parents may call you by a domestic name or your wife by any other address. While you are one, you are called by many addresses. Similarly God is one, but He has different names, different images, different rituals in different languages and regions. So it is foolish to fight over such petty issues.

"Follow your belief, have faith in it, but destroying others' opinion will lead to reaction of action and such a religious struggle will take the nation and society to its downfall.

"I have come to spread the message of unity and love, non-violence and brotherhood. Try all this once. Our ancestors were one, our past was one. Our present enmity and narrow-mindedness have divided us, while our future lies in living together and not quarrelling. Our ancestors have shown us the path of dialogue to resolve our disputes and differences. The ancient tradition of debate has resolved so many disputes over the centuries...this path is open even today. Those who want to prove the superiority of their views should do so through discussion. Is victory through arms and ammunition to conquer cities and kingdoms worth your while? You should ponder over it calmly and decide."

The meeting is suspended and the audience returns home, grasping their own meaning through their own understanding. Some agree; some disagree and a few have no opinion, either in favour or against as they are preoccupied with their own domestic concerns. They are delighted to see the sage who can kill the demon Ugra Bhairav and whose teachings are able to eliminate sorrows from life.

This group of foot-travellers now reaches the Gokarna shrine located on the sea-coast of Karnataka. The ancient pilgrim city eagerly awaits him. News about the vigour and popularity of his sermons has already reached here. Devotees throng to welcome him. He gets delayed in reaching the holy Shiva shrine in Gokarna but a smile plays on his calm and radiant face. He accepts the greetings of the people with affection while his disciples are worried about their *guru* who has not eaten yet. The *guru* however is happy giving *darshan* to the devotees and giving answers to their queries. Seeing his happiness and cheerfulness, no person can think of the long journey that he has undertaken without taking a morsel of food or a drop of water to drink. His objective is to first visit and worship Lord Gokarneshwar and subsequently think about food. However his disciples take the help of the temple managers and persuade the Acharya to weave his way from amidst the crowd to the temple's sanctum.

Entering the sanctorum, Acharya is mesmerised to see the beautiful statue of Ardhanarishvara. He begins to offer his prayers and the waves of his melodious notes reverberate in the sanctorum. The priests of the temple and their assistants are overcome with a strange and unique feeling of emotion.

The grand idol of Ardhanarishvara looks so alive today that the presence of both Shiva and Parvati can be felt. Everyone feels the flow of a divine energy in their veins. Acharya and his disciples perform a ritual worship of Lord Gokarna before they are guided from the sanctorum to the dining hall.

After a delicious meal, Acharya is escorted to his resting place. A huge crowd on both sides of the road looks with awe and curiosity at the teenage monk. It is difficult to tell whether the devotees are more or the spectators are more in number, but whoever sees him feels an intense feeling of fascination for him. Wherever he looks, the spectators forget themselves momentarily and feel a magnetic attraction. But then, exceptions are present everywhere and so is the case in Gokarna too! Gokarna is not an ordinary city; it is a city where the tradition of devotion and knowledge has not been broken since ancient times.

After performing the duty of welcoming the guests, the scholars of Gokarna eagerly look forward to holding a debate with Acharya. The *guru* is already prepared because the prime aim of his journey is to debate. But can they dare to debate with Acharya?

The list of those seeking to debate grows short when they hear about the defeat of Shankar's adversaries and eventually only one name is left. This is the name of Neelkanth, who is the author of many texts as the head of Shaivism. His intellectual power has been established in this area since long. Over the years, his disciple

Haridatta has also earned fame and popularity. Neelkanth had also given a commentary on *Brahmasutra* according to Shaivism and that too had become popular and was canonised.

Today evening, Acharya's debate has been fixed with this senior scholar named Neelkanth. When the sun sets in the west, people start gathering to hear their Shaivite scholar, Acharya Neelkanth in the debate hall but to their dismay, they witness their icon Neelkanth's defeat and who happily accepts the discipleship of the young Acharya, along with other disciples. Now they are ardent warriors of the victorious vehicle of monism. On the suggestion of Sanandan, Shankar takes leave from Gokarna to move towards a new destination, which is popularly known as Harihara pilgrimage centre. The entire city of Gokarna turns up to bid him farewell. Sanandan notices that at the time of the farewell, all those who are present, right from the priests of the temple to the cleaning staff, would have to face double the workload as a result of Acharya's visit.

By the time they reach Harihar *tirtha*, the sun has set. After their regular evening prayers, the group of religious warriors reach the entrance of the city, where they are welcomed with great pomp and show. They are taken to the holy Harihar temple in a procession. People from all walks of life look down from their roofs to behold and get fascinated at the sight of the charming teenage monk. At some places, flowers are sprinkled on them on the way while at a few places, gold and silver coins are offered.

On reaching the Harihar temple, Acharya and his disciples bow their heads in obeisance and the priests take them to the sanctorum. Those who get to see the wonderful statue of Hari and Har installed in the sanctorum consider themselves very lucky.

Acharya Shankar is surpised to see this conjoined incarnation of Vishnu and Shiva. He feels as if he has found an effective cure against the germs of ideological narrow-mindedness in the holy land of India. The doctrine of monism, which he has been promoting for years, finds a precise and practical foundation in his mind. Monism is not a core intellectual concept in this temple, but a revered ideal that can be felt with the touch and seen with the eye.

In different parts of India, the foolish ones who give their lives and take otlhers' lives in the name of their respective gods and goddesses can now understand from Lord Harihar that Lord Vishnu and Lord Shiva are not two separate entities but are one – they are two forms of one God. The animosity between their devotees is a product of their own foolishness and arrogance. Acharya reverently immerses himself in the magnificence of the wonderful form. The unique aspect of the wonderful statue of Lord Vishnu and Lord Shiva is that if you look at it from the left side, Vishnu is seen and if you look from the right side, then Lord Shiva is seen. Anyone who beholds gets awestruck. While taking delight in the beauty of the idol with devotion, a wonderful song springs from Acharya Shankar's lips in Sanskrit, which is considered the language of gods.

The song too is two-dimensional like the statue. Those who are worshippers of Lord Shiva find it to be an eulogy in praise of Lord Shiva: "O, the bearer of the sacred River Ganga, who provides nectar to the deities without any regret and who accepts the beautiful idol of the temple, O Narayan with immense form, bless me."

One after the other, the verse casts a miraculous impact on the devotees, taking them to new spiritual heights where all distinctions between man and man are erased; only supreme peace remains.

As the enchanted origin of this wonderful hymn in combined praise of Shiva and Vishnu is accomplished, there is a supreme silence for a few moments as if everyone has gone in a trance. It takes time to descend to the earth from such spiritual heights, so it takes time here too.

After conducting the rites and rituals, Acharya along with his disciples moves towards the holy temple of Ambika Devi located at a short distance. The indomitable energy of this tireless traveller is transferred to his disciples as no one seems tired and none demands rest or food. He carries the message of God in the form of a hymn and that serves as food.

From village to village, lane to lane, reducing the distances, breaking down the walls of discrimination and ignorance, this group of monks walks unceasingly every day, uniting the whole nation in one thread of emotions. Whether it is rocky roads or muddy pits, their journey does not stop. Like a swift river, they continue to flow while their footprints become indelible. Their signatures on the nation's consciousness may fade in the coming centuries like the names on the plates in duststorms, but when the watchman of time wipes away the dust, they are bound to shine again.

They have not come to break; they have come to connect. They do not let anyone to be defeated, just as the ocean does not conquer the rivers, but absorbs them with respect. They never quibble, never lie and never humiliate anyone. So the family of their ideology continuously increases. Villages, towns, cities, provinces – all are waking up to this cool breeze of intellectual awakening. Shankar speaks the language of harmony and love.

□

39

Mookambika Devi

Acharya Shankar's disciples and volunteers make their way through the crowd. Acharya with the simple desire to visit Mookambika reaches the door of the temple at Kollur. A crowd is seen moving like waves, but the unaffected Acharya, immersed in devotion, enters the temple.

The priests welcome him with chants and the idol of Goddess Mookambika in the sanctum appears to have come alive in his presence. Shankar, deep in devotional emotion, prostrates at the feet of the mother goddess and for a few moments remains still in the same posture on the ground. His disciples too follow their *guru*. After a few moments of calm and quiet worship, everyone gets up and begins to move out from the temple premises, though, like at other places, hawthorns of obstruction and protest also greet them.

The first of the messengers offers salutation to Acharya Shankar and says in a humble voice, "Your Majesty, this place is blessed with the best of learned men. Since ancient times, it hs been the Sharda Math (the seat of Mother Goddess). We want a self-realised and eminent scholar like you to be seated on this *peeth* (pedestal), but, for this, you have to win the local scholarly board through debate. Sir..." he clears his throat and continues, "till today no scholar has left as a winner from this place."

Acharya replies softly, "I accept your invitation. I am ready for the debate."

The messenger returns taking Acharya's answer while

Acharya and his companions take lunch and rest. They wait for the place and time of the debate in the guesthouse of the temple. A messenger arrives to inform the rules of the debate and the venue being the Knowledge Pavilion of Sharda Peeth.

After the night's rest, the morning rays spread their glory to announce the beginning of the next day. There is an assembly of scholars, princes, devotees and spectators in Sharda Peeth. Even before the appointed time, the debate venue gets overcrowded.

With the blowing of conch shell, Acharya enters the auditorium. People are taken in by his large eyes, raised forehead, buoyant face and tightly sculpted body. Some are satisfied at his fair complexion, while some are enchanted at his large eyes. The local scholars feel that this young monk with his handsome personality has conquered the auditorium even without speaking.

As soon as the judge sits down, the Acharya also goes and occupies the reserved seat. His disciples also sit down behind him. On the other side, the opposite party comprising passionate scholars take their seats.

The debate is inaugurated with the promulgation of statutory notices and rules. A reputed scholar from the opposite side, while ridiculing monism, describes God and beings as two entities. They claim angrily, "Sir, you think you are the only scholar left in this world while the rest are fools because according to your understanding, there is no difference between a devotee and God.

"You have proved that since Brahma, Vishnu and Mahesh are illusionary, your principle of formless monism is true. It has no hands, no legs; therefore it is formless. Since it is formless, it is true and the one who is with bodily form is unreal. Hail your knowledge!" they mock ironiocally.

Shankar calmly replies, "O great scholars! Since centuries, the victory of knowledge has always been certain; it does not need the shelter of your rebuke.

So far as there is a dispute between the corporeal and the

formless, it is intellectual luxury for scholars like you. God is omnipotent and that's why he is not bound to any form. One who is limited in size cannot be God because God is infinite. He is both corporeal and formless."

His scintillating voice echoes amidst the perfect silence in the assembly. "Monism is not my invention; it is prevalent in the *Vedas, Shrutis, Upanishad and* elsewhere. Monism has no dispute with the other doctrines. Just as scholars like the rivers merge in the ocean, similarly all sects ultimately reach the great gateway to monism.

"The best scholars, devotees and God are one because father and son are one. Their faces, gestures, bodily postures are same or with the passage of time become one. Similarly, the soul is born from the Supreme Soul; therefore, the soul-and Supreme Soul are one. Just as there is no difference between the seed and the crop, in the same manner, the soul that is born from the Supreme is a small replica of it. This is monism."

The adjudicator gives the opponent an opportunity for counter-argue but the opposition has nothing to say. His scholarship melts like wax in front of the Acharya's fire of truth. He accepts his defeat.

Another group of scholars comes forward. They begin by launching an interrogative attack but Acharya does not get distracted by this. He utters with clarity, "God is omnipresent; He is present everywhere like air. He is in Brahma, Vishnu, Mahesh, Durga, Lakshmi, Saraswati and also in living beings. The differences in its shape and form are nothing but folly.

"That imperishable God is pervasive in every particle of Nature.The entire creation is his form which pervades in rivers, trees, vegetation, houses, constellations, land, desert, sky, space and everywhere. Any high or low, any discrimination is nothing but a mental disorder.

"Violence against any living being is violence against the Supreme Soul. Therefore, bloodshed between Shaivas and

Vaishnavas or Buddhists and Sanatanis is fanaticism; not religion."

Acharya patiently gives evidence from scriptures and disarms his opponents. As soon as the opposing party accepts defeat, the judge declares the victory of Acharya. All the scholars accept Acharya as their *guru*. The assembly hall resonates with their cheers.

The group of scholars, who was eager to debate with him, now requests him to be seated on the Sharda Peeth. Acharya sits down on it with ease. This incident is propagated in the city by the witnesses to this debate.

□

40

Sringeri's Shri Bali

The success story of Acharya spreads consistently over days and nights. In Mookambika, devotees gather to acquire knowledge for three days. Acharya quenches their thirst for knowledge but the hearts of the people are not satiated. He promises to visit them again before departing.

On the way to Shringeri, he has to pass through *agrahara* (endowment) named Shri Bali which was an ancient *agrahara*. Two thousand Brahmin families lived here at that time. All these Brahmins were very religious. In the morning hours, the fragrant, holy smoke emerging from the holy incense fire is seen billowing out from all the houses to the chanting of hymns. Sri Bali's Brahmins are reputed for observing Vedic rituals.

The Brahmins of this endowment are highly impressed with the fame and talent of the great commentator, Mandan Mishra. They warmly welcome him and his team, especially Mandan Mishra. Mango-leaf hangings are decorated on the streets of the village. The women sprinkle flowers from their homes; the men offer fresh flower garlands. Amid cheers, Mandan visits the temple of Shiva-Parvati in the endowment.

The Brahmins of Shri Bali become ecstatic on seeing Mandan Mishra, who is then under the guardian umbrella of the *guru's* affection. Even the slightest shadow of defeat is not visible in his personality. The golden talent of his personality has become as bright as gold by serving the *guru*. He understands that the limits to his future duties are much more than the limits of Mahishmati city on the banks of River Narmada. It is by the grace of his *guru* that he is evolving from a drop to an ocean.

The sun is now about to cross the boundaries of Aryavart with the complete victory of Acharya. His name is to shine in the entire nation. He only remembers his new life, new name, new way of life and new dream; the old one he has left behind in Mahishmati to be never recollected again. He is a monk now; he is Sureshvara, the beloved disciple of his *guru*. Sureshvara is highly respected by the other scholars as well. Each one acknowledges the fact that even Acharya Shankar respects him for his wisdom. His advice is mandatory at the time of important decisions.

In Shri Bali, while Sureshvara is seated in meditation outside Acharya's room, he notices a couple coming with their teenage son. He recalls that the news of the miracle that had brought the dead child alive during their stay in Mookambika has reached this endowment. When the couple draws near and expresses their desire to visit Acharya, Sureshvara stops them and inquires about their motive.

The man comes forward and introduces himself, "I am Prabhakar, a Brahmin. I have studied scriptures too but I am very sad that my son is dumb and cannot speak."

Sureshvara affectionately consoles him and as soon as he receives Acharya's permission, Prabhakar asks the man along with his son and wife to be allowed to meet his *guru*.

While greeting the Acharya seated on the throne, Pandit Prabhakar places coconut, sweets, etc. at his feet and says with folded hands, "O great scholar, this is my only son, who is thirteen-years old and still underdeveloped. He neither speaks nor eats, not even plays; he does not have any childlike qualities. He remains indifferent like an old man. Due to this, we are very sad. By the grace of God, I have enough money, good health and respect in the society but this is to no avail. Please save him by giving your blessings."

The child's mother entreats, "O Lord, you have revived the

dead child in Mookambika; please make our only child healthy and normal."

Acharya looks at the teenager after listening to the request of the parents. The child appeared to be goodlooking, brilliant and sharp, while in terms of behaviour, he looked dumb. Acharya's vision has seen that the child is not a fool. He asks the boy in the midst of a crowd of parents and visitors, waiting for a miracle, "O child, who are you? Whose son are you and what is your name? Where are you going and where have you come from? Seeing you makes my heart happy. Introduce yourself."

The mute boy, who had remained silent since birth, replies in a very sweet voice, "Neither am I a human being nor a deity nor a demigod or a priest. I am nether a warrior, a merchant, an outcast, a celibate, a family person. I am not even a hermit or a monk. I am only a soul, the embodiment of self-realisation."

His parents and neighbours were shocked to hear the child speak. The child, who had never spoken a single word so far, was describing the nature of the soul in a beautiful Sanskrit verse, "Thanks, thanks! The glory of Acharya Shankar cannot be surpassed!" hail all in a storm of cheers and joy.

The grateful parents emotionally drop to their knees in front of the Acharya. He raises them affectionately and places his hand on the child in blessing. He says to Prabhakar Pandit, "Sir, this child must have been a perfect *yogi* in his previous birth. He is neither retarded nor dumb, but being very high, above all worldliness, he keeps on drinking the divine flavour by remaining absorbed in Satchidananda."

The child's parents are taken aback on hearing this and tears flow down their eyes. After all, this child is their child and howsoever he is, he is dear to them. They had brought him up by pampering him. How could they hand over the apple of their eyes to a monk?

They take their child home after bowing to Acharya Shankar. The boy keeps insisting on going to meet the Acharya the entre night. The husband and wife spend the night, keeping awake due to worry.

In the morning, the mother hugs her son and begs him to call her 'Mother', but the child refuses despite repeated pleadings. The child keeps on insisting that he wants to go to Acharya. He does not even touch his food or water. The helpless couple again seek shelter at the feet of Acharya. The mother of the child falls at Acharya's feet and weeps, "O sage, please make my son normal and healthy. How will I live without him? Kindly provide us relief from our sorrow by altering his mind and thoughts."

Hearing the mother's cries and prayers, the Acharya consoles her affectionately and says, "In the body of your son resides an intense ascetic because of which he is not really your son. You are mourning for him in vain. If you calm your mind and remember the sequence of events after his birth, then perhaps you will realise the truth and the reality."

Acharya's speech is laced with love and compassion.The unhappy couple tries to become calm and recall that when this child was born, both of them had taken him to the hut of an ascetic who lived on the banks of River Yamuna. They had laid him in that cottage and gone to bathe in the river. The ascetic was engaged in meditation. When the child woke up, he began to cry and kick his hands and legs frantically as a result of which he slipped into the river. By the time the parents could run towards him, the child drowned in the river and died. Weeping and wailing, they went to the ascetic's hut with his body. Moved at their sorrow, the ascetic meditated and the boy became alive. They took him back home but before returning, they tried to thank the ascetic. They were not aware that the ascetic was in a deep trance and unaware of their words.

On recollecting the entire sequence of events in their mind, the couple understood everything. They accepted their destiny and with a sad heart returned to their world by handing over their son to Acharya.

The very next day in the *ashram*, the child is initiated into becoming a monk by reciting the scriptures. Acharya names him Hastamalak, meaning 'for whom the knowledge of Brahman is as clear and easy as a gooseberry on his hand'.

Hastamalak's natural talent lies in spirituality and his self-knowledge is about to become more intense after being freed from the worldly obstacles. Even in his adolescence, he had been very wise. With his arrival, there is now more joy among the disciples. They move around with enthusiasm on the journey. The general public too is keen to behold such a young monk.

By now, people of all age groups have joined the disciples' circle. Sureshvara is oldest in age; then come Acharya and Sanandan who are of the same age while Hastamalak is the youngest and all the others are counted in the middle of them, i.e. older than Hastamalak and younger than Sureshvara.

This unique group of monks, immersed in the bliss of Vedanta, marches towards Shringeri under the leadership of Acharya Shankar.

□

41
Adornment of Shringeri

The ancient Shringpur is the present-day Shringeri, which is a sacred and picturesque place lying in the plateau of the famous Western Ghats of India. The sight of the holy River Tunga, descending from the Mount Rishya Shringa and the gusts of fresh air blowing in from the dense forests captivate even the detached monks. While trudging amid the tall trees like skyscrapers, the monks can only feel the silence of the forest apart from their footsteps on the dry leaves and the chirping of birds. Now some distance away, they can see the thick clumps of trees disappear and the plains appear.

After crossing the fields, they notice a small reservoir of water formed by rainwater rolling down the mountains. Here the green grassland and the place provide the shade of some trees.

Acharya Shankar walks in the front at his fast pace. He waits a few moments for his disciples following behind to catch up with him. His eyes fall on a pregnant frog which is feeling restless due to the heat of the sun. It is given shade by a black cobra under its huge hood. Acharya is left speechless at this strange yet beautiful sight. His heart decides to make this holy place his hermitage as it is not only endowed with natural beauty but also is the place where Sage Rishya Shringa of the *Ramayana* era had done penance. Rishya Shringa, son of Sage Vibhandak, had a horn on his head since birth. It is said that he was born from the womb of a deer. His father Vibhandak himself had to take care of the baby. He raised him in solitude.

Rishya Shringa had never seen any other man except his father. He used to indulge in severe penance night and day under the guidance of his father. Once a famine raged in the neighbouring kingdom. The king, on the advice of his scholars, invited Sage Rishya Shringa to pray for rain to come to his kingdom. Untouched by worldly contact, when Rishya Shringa saw the beautiful maidens who had come to invite him, he was overcome with emotions. He felt intense attraction towards them. The maidens left after the invitation but Rishya Shringa's mind became restless and disturbed. He resolved to leave his hermitage and reach the famine-ridden state, where he was given a grand welcome. With his arrival, it started to rain in the state. When the water crisis ended, both the king and the subjects became so grateful to the sage that the king married his daughter Shanta to Sage Rishya Shringa. Later, he received an invitation from Dashrath, the emperor of Ayodhya to participate in the *kameshti yagya* (the *yajna* to bear a child). His blessings fulfilled King Dashrath's wish and he was blessed with four distinguished sons. Even in the midst of the hospitality offered at the palace, the sage remembered his place of worship and finally returned there. At the same place of Sage Rishya Shringa, a new pilgrimage site begins to take shape with the efforts of Acharya Shankar.

Even before Acharya reaches Shringeri, the Chalukya king sends his emissaries to make the necessary arrangements. He diligently gets facilities arranged for the monks by constructing huts for them to reside in.

The devotees now begin to visit Acharya regularly as soon as they come to know about his stay in Shringeri. In this new *ashram*, the day begins with the recitation of Vedic hymns and the holy fragrance of the ingredients burnt in the *yajna*. A Sanskrit school is inaugurated for children and adolescents; *ashrams* are prepared for the visiting devotees and daily sacks of food are filled in the granary. Farmers, traders, princes and the common people – all make donations to the *ashram* as per each's capacity.

Articles like food, clothes, sweets, dry fruits, gold and silver coins are collected in plenty. Those who are given the responsibility of doing this work have no time left at their disposal.

Three days later arrives the auspicious occasion when Acharya is set to establish Goddess Sharda on the rocks in the middle of RiverTunga. The craftsmen get busy carving artifacts of Shri Yantra on the rock while carpenters are engaged in carving a beautiful statue of the goddess on the ripened sandalwood in the workshop built near Acharya's hut. They work efficiently in solitude with the aim of carving a lively statue of the goddess.

As usual, Acharya is preaching in the discourse hall with his disciples and devotees. He is throwing light on the future outline of the *ashram*. "We are going to consecrate this place by erecting the idol of the mother of all, the Goddess of Power and prosperity. With the hard work of all and the donations of the donors, the supreme power, Mother Sharda, would be established in the form of a *guru*.

"In the coming times, this place will take the shape of a pilgrimage centre owing to its purity, divine experience and craftsmanship. Shri Sharda will be seated here on Shri Chakra, from where the waves of prosperity and joy, of devotion and knowledge, of hard work and penance will flow, not only for the benefit of the whole nation, but the entire humanity."

The pavilion bursts into applause from the devotees. On the appointed date and time, the sandalwood idol, comprising three fundamental features of Nature (*trigunatmak*), of Mother Sharda is established. The day of consecration becomes an occasion for a festival for innumerable people. Countless and endless lines of visitors attend the sessions of hymns and food. When the main worship of the goddess is accomplished with the recitation of *Lalita Sahastranaam*, the whole atmosphere turns divine. The sound of conch shell resonates in all directions.

The newly built *ashram* of Acharya Shankar slowly develops into a regular religious monastery. He establishes a temple of Kal

Bhairav on the eastern hill of Shringeri, a temple for Anjaneya on the western hill, a temple for Durga on the southern hill and ae temple of Kali on the northern hill. There is a regular construction and consecration of idols in the temples of many gods and goddesses within the premises of the monastery. The campus is constantly expanding. Innumerable deities of gods like Vishnu, Bhuvaneshwari, Rama, Brahma, Hanuman, Garun, Shaligram, Chandramoulishvara, Ratnagarbha, Ganapati, etc. are placed here.

The universal vision of Acharya Shankar binds everyone with one thread. Now remains the unique effort of binding the society divided into classes. Shri Sharda is the main goddess in this monastery, but due care has been taken to include the local folk-deities, local sages and other lesser known deities. It seems as if the new message of coordination overpowers the lamps fuelled by the narrow-mindedness and hatred-centred communitarianism. In Shringeri, Sanatan Dharma seems to be renewing itself after wiping away the dust of the ages.

The wave of intellectual revolution has spread and reached Shringeri. It is connecting man with man, thought with thought and sect with sect. Not only the Shaivas and Vaishnavas, but even the Shaktas and Arihants have understood the message of coordination and tolerance. The bright future is clearly visible in this message of coordination, tolerance and co-existence, not only to the merchants and entrepreneurs, but also to the soldiers and rulers.

If there is peace, the farmers will do farming and the merchants will do trade. The craftsmen, the teachers, the common masses – all are fed up with the ongoing worthless religious conflicts and wars. The message of non-violence and peace is attracting them. That's why the crowd in Shringari is increasing day and night. Acharya is trying to build a new society and restoring Sanatan Dharma to its original glory in a planned manner. Everything in the *ashram* is systematic, pre-planned and disciplined. Here one can never be arrogant or lethargic. Acharya himself works hard and the same is true of his disciples. All the monks in the monastery wake up in the wee hours. Their spiritual practices are not halted even for a moment. The various activities and tasks, like reception, accommodation, food, worship, cleanliness, agriculture, finance and education are clearly distributed among the disciples and volunteers. The three activities mandatory for all are reading, teaching and hard work. The responsibilities for worshipping the deities are of varied types. From sunrise to sunset, everyone performs his assigned duties. The night hours are fixed for specific spiritual practice and relaxation.

The regular, systematic and transparent functioning of Shringeri Ashram have built trust among the public. Endless pupils come to the *ashram* every day to visit and get initiated by Acharya Shankar.They wait patiently in long queues.

Every afternoon, Acharya Shankar delivers discourses on public education, sitting on an open platform. A large crowd hears him to find solution to the complex social and religious issues. After the discourse, he replies to queries of the audience.

The programme completes with the distribution of *prasad*.

The monastery is developing as a centre of spiritual uplift in the society through sacrifice, penance, self-study and spiritual practice. People are inspired by the ideal lifestyle of Acharya and so they are joining him in large numbers.

Acharya has also been writing texts and commentaries. like *Vivek Chudamani, Bodhsaar, Vedanta Kesari, Sarvadarshan Siddhanta*, etc. to give impetus to his intellectual movement and to aid in religious teaching of his disciples. His every moment is dedicated to action. In this campaign of religious integration and renaissance, the number of devotees coming from far north, east and west India are increasing. There is an influx of devotees from distant places like Benaras, Mithila, Gaur, Magadha, Vatsa, Kaushal, Anga, etc.

This region boasts of Kerala, Chola, Pallavas and Chalukyas. People coming from the north are astonished to see that the responsibility of the *ashram*, which has been set up in such a remote place in the south, is in the hands of Sureshvara, who hails from the city of Mahishmati. He is the doer and the creator here. Apart from him, the chief priests of many temples have accompanied Acharya from eastern and western India. Merit and loyalty are given more importance in the *ashram*. The respect for local is equally taken care of; there is no favouritism.

After his discourse in the evening, Acharya affectionately calls Sureshvara and clears the doubts in the minds of other disciples. He says, "I wish that instead of writing the *vartika*, you should write such a treatise on monism that all unnecessary doubts may be resolved."

Sureshvacharya takes his *guru's* order to his head and heart. Then, in front of all, the *guruji* lovingly orders and tells Padmapada, "I know Padmapada, your wish is to compose the *vartika*, but you write a commentary on *Sutra-Bhashya* as you can express your opinion well on that."

Padmapada promptly begins to follow his *guru's* wish. Acharya Shankar's *ashram* is a unique centre of knowledge and science. Here every major disciple is engaged in some specified work. Acharya himself is writing commentaries on several major religious texts; Sureshvara is engrossed in writing treatises on monism; Padmapada in composing the commentary on *Sutra Bhashya*, Ananda Giri is writing commentaries on the *Upanishads*. The same is true of other prominent disciples. Life here is full of hard work and the specific responsibility assigned does not relieve one from regular responsibilities. Programmes like prayers, hymns, worship, meditation, reading, recitation, discourse, daily events, meeting with the masses, etc. are conducted on a regular basis.

In the busy schedule at the *ashram*, the moment of celebration comes when someone completes a book. On that day, after the discourse of the *guru*, there is an announcement about the completion of the composition of the new book.The author is made to deliver a lecture. The other scholars critically appreciate the work. In the end, Acharya gives his blessings and the creator is honoured.

Today a moment of such celebaration has come after strenuous work in the monastery. Suresh's writing talent has blossomed and is there for all to see. He has dedicated the scripture *Naishyakarma Siddhi* at the feet of the *guru*. Acharya Shankar is seated gracefully in the discourse hall on his seat. Sureshvara is seated on one side and Padmapada on the other, near his feet. Anandagiri and Totakacharya are seated below the stage with their respective disciples.

Trusted and dedicated devotees, who come to hear the daily discourses of Acharya Shankar, are also seated with reverence. Today's sermon is over. Queries of the audience and students have also been answered. There will now be public recitations of extracts from literature composed by Sureshvaracharya and Padmapada. The programme director invites Sureshvaracharya to speak about his work.

Acharya Shankar's face is as usual, shining with extraordinary brilliance. One can feel the aura of divine ecstasy on his countenance. Sureshvara, sitting humbly at the *guru's* feet, stands up and starts speaking, "Dear brothers and students, this book is a result of the *guru's* grace. The existence of monism does not need any explanation. Just as the sun is not introduced, similarly the rays of monism reach everywhere. It was beyond my capacity to calculate these rays. I have tried to express the ultimate truth in my broken language by the *guru's* bliss. Whatever it is, it is his glory and therefore it is dedicated to him."

Acharya Shankar's speech contlnues in the midst the joyful cheers of the audience, "My dear *atman*, you are all a part of the same imperishable Supreme Being. In this book, dear Sureshvara has explained the wonderful concept of monism with his extraordinary intelligence. I am extremely pleased with this. I am sure that his skilful writing will be articulated in many great texts in the times to come. When you people will look at this interesting book, its depth will take you to the core of spirituality. My countless blessings are upon him.

"I take great pleasure today to mention the commentary written by my dear Padmapada. Padmapada, the four chapters you have just written are comprehensive and substantive. My desire is that you may soon complete it. This creation will be for the welfare of society and will receive appreciation from all. My countless blessings are with you."

Excerpts from these compositions are publicly recited amidst cheers and joyful sounds. Scholars freely assess the merits of the work. It seems as if Goddess Saraswati keeps pouring her blessings continuously in Shringeri. There is a continuous performance of this *yajna* of knowledge. Here hearts are filled with generosity, the mind is free and the soul wanders in spiritual heights, but for ordinary people it is a holy pilgrimage where there are magnificent idols in the temples, a divine atmosphere, a confluence of *tunga* and *bhadra*, and amid the shadow of natural beauty, it has an affectionate association with Acharya.

The crowd of devotees never lessens. From north, south, east and west, this place attracts the seekers of truth like a magnet. Shaivas, Vaishnavas, Shaktas, formless, atheists, reclused are all drawn to this site. A new society, an all-pervading, all-encompassing Sanatan concept is finding a revival here, dispelling disputes and differences in the cool waters of River Tungabhadra.

Groups of young saints are engaged in contemplating, undertaking research and innovating subjects of their interests. During the journey, some of the senior talents, who were engaged in penance and meditation in their respective regions, have gathered here under the spell of the magnetic personality of Acharya. They are giving guidance and cooperation in the experiments conducted here. A unique project of scientific practices under the shadow of religion is being conducted here in the Shri Ram temple of Ayodhya. Along with *'Buddham sharanam gacchami'*, the chants of *'Ram, Ram, Sita Ram'* can also be heard in Ayodhya.

After the unique success of Ayodhya, Acharya's victory procession starts to move towards Gaya, the ancient pilgrimage centre got conveying the message of co-ordination, cooperation and love to Mithila, Magadha, Nalanda, Rajgriha by chanting the *mantra* of monism in the ears of the public.

Mithila, which was once illuminated under the majesty of the royal sage, like Videh Raj Janak, has now come under the influence of Buddha's magical message. Magadha, Nalanda, Rajgriha were already the admirers of Tathagata! The roots of Buddhism were already strong here. These areas had seen Buddha with their own eyes and had heard him with their ears. In every age, the subjects of the warring kings heaved a sigh of relief on hearing Buddha's message of peace. Today, when Acharya Shankar has come on the same soil, the age-old memories seem to come alive.

The villagers and citizens who have seen Acharya everywhere in Magadha, Nalanda, Rajgriha are reminded of Lord Buddha. They exclaim, "Ah! What a splendid personality, beautiful body, glowing face with an enlightened aura, dazzling eyes, intense and loving voice that cools the ears! One who sees becomes enchanted and whoever hears, feels his intimacy in his heart."

Gautam Buddha too had the same impressive personality. Owing to his speech and personality, he had completely conquered the complex and fragmented society of India. Now the same responsibility is placed on the young shoulders of Acharya Shankar. Gautam Buddha had uprooted the distortions that had entered into the Vedic religion, but when the enthusiasm and arrogance of his disciples decided to eradicate the Eternal, the same Divine authority this time had come in the role of Acharya Shankar to re-establish the truth of life.

In this act of giving new life to the everlasting culture through his victory procession, the next halt is at the ancient pilgrimage centre of Gaya. Since ages, the followers of Vedic culture, from every corner of India, have been visiting Gaya *dham* for the salvation of their ancestors. The *Gadadhara* form of Lord Vishnu is worshipped in Gaya since ancient times. It is the sacred duty of every son to donate the *pinda* with devotion in Gaya. The *pindadan* (homage to departed soul) is compulsory for the salvation of one's ancestors. That is why Gaya has always been the main centre of pilgrimage as well as the centre for carrying on the tradition of charity in Vedic culture.

Gautam Buddha attained enlightenment under the Bodhi tree near Gaya. So the place became famous as 'Bodh Gaya' in a way that both the importance and dignity of ancient Gaya is maintained. Emperor Ashoka had enshrined a statue of Mahatma Buddha in a grand and magnificent temple at Bodh Gaya. Since then, Bodh Gaya has become the most essential and holiest pilgrimage for Buddhists all over the world. In practice, Bodh Gaya is a symbol of the authority and power of Buddhism, the religion of Buddha.

At this same Bodh Gaya, when Acharya Shankar reaches, holding the victory flag of monism, an unknown tension and fear grips the minds of the Buddhists. Acharya's fame had spread as an anti-Buddhist and as supporter of the *Vedas*. Some Buddhists wait impatiently for Acharya Shankar to speak against Lord Gautam Buddha or the path propounded by him so that they could voice their strong opposition! Some who were more zealous stand ready with stones, sticks, balls in case the logic falls short, then violence can be adopted.

On reaching Bodh Gaya, Acharya first of all visits the Buddhist temple. He bows down reverently in front of the statue of Lord Buddha. The chief priest is struck dumb to see that the Acharya, who was proclaimed to be anti-Buddha, is worshipping Buddha with deep devotion!

After saying his prayers, Acharya goes out. The Buddhists present in the temple courtyard greet him with courtesy and urge him to address the people present. Acharya begins to speak in his melodious voice. The noise and unrest inside and outside subsides as Acharya says, "I bow to the Supreme Lord residing in the soul of all of you in this holy temple of Lord Buddha, the ninth incarnation of Lord Vishnu. Lord Buddha has shown the path of liberation not only to our great land, but also to the entire humanity against the web of violence, malice, mutual conflict, enmity, high and low. His teachings have established the same values of equality as those of our great sages and ascetics who devoted their lives to penance."

There is a continous applause at each word that he utters. He firmly asserts, "The enmity between Vedic religion and Buddhism is baseless. Lord Buddha himself was a Sanatani and opposed the distortions in Vedic religion. It is a big mistake to consider him to be anti-Vedas..."

He asks, "Sanatan Dharma considers salvation as the aim of life while Buddha considered *nirvana* as the ultimate truth. Please tell me what is the difference between the two words? They are merely two words with a similar meaning."

With his eloquence, Acharya is successful in eradicating the doubts in the minds of of the Buddhists. Those who had collected stones and sticks to kill him are humbled as they bow down to take the soil at his feet. His declaration of Gautam Buddha as the ninth incarnation of Vishnu is strongly opposed by some hypocritical *pandits*; they even call him a 'disguised Buddhist', but the majority accept it as authentic. Sanatan Dharma followers also start worshipping Buddha and in turn, the Buddhists reconnect with their Sanatani identity. This successful attempt of national integration is repeated across the country. The new message of unity that came out of Bodh Gaya takes root across the country. The lifeless Sanatan establishments of Gaya are revived again in the presence of Acharya.

Taking a heartfelt farewell from Sanatani followers and Buddhists of Gaya, this eternal traveller now proceeds towards the land of Bengal.

□

42

Departure of Padmapada

Ever since Padmapada has read the *Naishkarmya Siddhi* by Sureshvaracharya, he has been feeling restless. He is overwhelmed to read such an interesting and impressive explanation of the monism doctrine. He was under the impression that Sureshvara had not become a disciple of *guruji* with his mind but had been pushed under compulsion on being defeated in debate. He so far believed that Sureshvara merely superficially showed his leanings towards Vedanta and monism but was not ritualistic at heart. He does not even like *guruji* but misused *guruji's* innate affection like so many other selfish and hypocritical people and due to which *guruji's* life had been threatened.

The importance given by *guruji* to Sureshvara pricks somewhere in his heart and that is why, when *guruji* entrusts the responsibility of creating the *vartik* to Sureshvara, he is unable to suppress his displeasure. After all, Padmapada feels that despite his knowledge, *sadhana* and devotion to *guruji*, the latter is more generous towards others. A feeling of neglect which had been overwhelmimg him since a long time now takes a form of sorrow due to its continuance. Even a splash of *guruji's* love cannot prevent the fire of sorrow from burning in his mind. □

43

Atonement of Padmapada

Padmapada starts reading the *Naishkarmya Siddhi* given by *guruji* with mixed feelings of sorrow and doubt. His state of mind changes as he proceeds reading the next few pages. It begins to appear as if Acharya Shankar himself has written this. Whatever delusions he has about Sureshvara soon dissipate like a cloud. Padmapada feels proud at *guruji's* wise vision. He wonders how *guruji's* transparent vision had seen the qualities which he himself could not see? He had been considering Sureshvara as his rival for no reason and had doubted the wisdom of *guruji*. He now wants to leave but where can he go? The night passes in thinking over his predicament and tossing and turning on his bed without sleeping. There is a feeling of atonement in his heart. The idea of pilgrimage has come to his mind for the enhancement of his mind and conduct. He goes towards *guruji's* hut, suppressing his anxiety.

He sees Acharya sitting in *padmasana* and is pleased to see his dear disciple Padmapada approach. He welcomes him by saying, "Come, son!"

Padmapada bows his head at his *guru's* feet to receive the blessings for his success. When *guruji* indicates to him to sit, Padmapada goes and sits down on the left to seek permission by saying, "*Guruji*, if you permit, I want to go on a pilgrimage."

Guruji replies, "Padmapada, staying close to the *guru* is the greatest pilgrimage for a disciple. Those whose conduct is pure become the centre of pilgrimage. Your conduct is so pure that you don't need to go on a pilgrimage. The acts of human welfare that you conduct in the *ashram* with dedication and hard work earn more merit than you would get from a pilgrimage. But if you insist on going on a pilgrimage, I bless you."

A new society begins to evolve at Shringeri with people speaking in different languages, like Marathi, Gujarati, Kannada, Malayalam, Tamil, Sanskrit, Bengali, etc. live together in harmony and feel alike under the umbrella of Vedanta. Shringeri is not merely a religious *ashram* or a school for studying Sanskrit text, but a centre where research and study are promoted in subjects like Ayurveda, Economics, Chemistry and Agriculture. Scholars with conflicting views live together. They are both fascinated and annoyed on learning how little they know of each other and that how many similarities are present among them; that truth does not have only one dimension. They begin to realise that food, hymns, language and dress of every place originate from the local elements and so the differences do not amount to enmity. The same God is present in everyone's soul. Hence, when there is any opposition, it is foolish to translate the differences of opinions into differences of hearts.

The confluence of knowledge, love and spirituality flows in this budding *ashram* at Shringeri. Whoever takes a bath in this confluence, feels energised with a new consciousness. All disputes, differences, moods, despair – everything dissolves in the purity of River Tungabhadra.

Padmapada reads out the opening part of the commentary on the *Sutrabhashya* to *guruji*. Acharya is deeply touched at the rendering by Padampada. He narrates the Vedanta so beautifully that *guruji* visualises Padmapada's success in future. Acharya appreciates Padmapada's work with affection and remarks, "Padmapada, you should complete this work soon. It will mark the victory flag of Vedanta. Thus I want you to name it as *Vijay-Dindim.*"

Padampada is filled with gratitude in his mind. He feels his agony flow out and erode in the stream of *guruji's* unceasing affection. He bows down to *guruji* and returns to his hut. Padmapada's disciples eagerly await his return. They hear the description of *guruji's* discussion from Padmapada's mouth and are are elated to embark on a pilgrimage.

After a few days, while leaving for the pilgrimage, the newly created *Vijay Dindim* is now in the hands of these pilgrims. Padmapada has seen affection in the form of a teardrops in the eyes of Acharya Shankar while granting him permission to leave. The same is the condition of Sureshwar, whom he has so far considered as his opponent.

Acharya affectionately bids him farewell for the journey by giving him important instructions related to morning and evening walk, protection against the sun and the travel route. Padmapada's and his disciples' throats become choked with emotions on leaving the *ashram* but they move forward towards their first destination.

□

44

Shakuni Uncle of Padmapada

The pilgrims set their goal to visit Rameshwaram. On the way, they visit the holy pilgrimage sites like Kaalsthali, Kanchipuram, Pundarikapuram, Shivaganga etc. Now they are moving towards Srirangam. Today is the eleventh day of the journey. Padmapada decides to stay at his maternal uncle's house with all the disciples since it is on their way. Every day they stay somewhere or the other. He discusses this matter with his disciples and no one objects as it does not go against the *sannyasi* religion.

Padmapada's maternal uncle is a staunch ritualist. At first, he does not recognise his nephew in a monk's robe and with his head tonsured and also because for many years his whereabouts were not known. But, when he recognises his nephew, he feels sad that his lost nephew has been found but as a monk! He decides to bring this misguided pilgrim back on the path of dualism. He makes good arrangements for food and rest for all the pilgrims.

After the meal, a meeting is decided upon. Uncle, who was a well-euipped dualist scholar and disciple of Mimansa Prabhakar, begins to argue against the renunciation of Padmapada. Soon, unknowingly the debate between monism and dualism gets converted into a battlefield of arguments between the nephew and the uncle. Uncle realises that it is not easy to defeat the nephew. Leaving the dispute in the middle, he snatches the *Vijay Dindim* from his nephew's hands and goes to his room to sit down to study it.

The pilgrims go to sleep with their *guru* and guide Padmapada, but the lamp in the study room of uncle continues to be lit even after midnight. Uncle has read the entire book in the last three or four hours and is bewildered when seen in the light of the lamp that illuminates the darkness on his face. He feels defeated after reading the book by Padmapada. He had so far been so proud of his *guru* Prabhakar and his intellect but today his nephew had put this pride in danger.

He fears that if this book becomes popular in the world, then monism would occupy a strong hold and dualism would get replaced. He makes up his mind to do his duty and falls into deep sleep. Early next morning, he places his hand on his nephew's head and says with affection, "Dear Padmapada, I am amazed at your skill. You have explained monism with such logic and authenticity that even an honest person like me is feeling disturbed today."

Padmapada is pleased to hear his praise from his uncle's lips and feels proud at the kindness shown. After rejoicing in the affection of his uncle, the pilgrim Padmapada leaves his book behind for the benefit of his uncle and gladly accepts to take it back on his return.

When Padmapada returns with his disciples with renewed enthusiasm after paying a visit to Rameshwaram and the holy Setubandha shrine, he finds that his uncle's house has been burned to ash. Uncle has taken shelter in the temple. Padmapada goes to the temple where his uncle bursts into tears and says, "Son, in a sudden fire, I have lost everything. I am sorry that I could not even save your book."

Padmapada is shocked to hear this and feels cheated. He repents at his stupidity at leaving behind the book he had created with such arduous labour. Now with what face will he be able to face his *guru*?

He notices the agony on his uncle's face and forgets about his own sorrow at the loss. He consoles his uncle and with the help of his disciples works day and night to restore his uncle's house.

He now feels an overpowering urge for Acharya's affection. Taking leave from his uncle, he and his disciples walk towards Shringeri to meet Acharya. After a day's journey, he reaches a village in the evening. He is told by travellers from Shringeri that Acharya had left the town to go to his birthplace, Kaladi, a few days ago.

Padmapada is pleased to get this information after having been away from the *ashram* for six long months. The travellers narrate that the prestige of Shringeri has been increasing day by day with devotees, the curious and the common people from all over the country constantly arriving at Shringeri to meet Acharya. Shringeri has now come to witness an atmosphere of celebration, be it a sunny day or a rainy one. It has become the favourite place to visit for meritorious and studious youth because Shringeri has now become the site where all the arts flourish in the *ashram* under the guidance of the best teachers.

Padmapada knows that this marks only the beginning and that his great *guru* has been planning to set up several energy centres like Shringeri across the country.

Devotees returning from Shringeri are very pleased to see Padmapada as they had heard that Padmapada was the first and foremost disciple of Acharya Shankar and was very much like his *guru*. They appreciate their good fortune at this sudden and unprecedented meeting with Padampada and consider it a valuable gift.

Padmapada resumes his journey the next morning – not to Shringeri, but to Kerala.

□

45

Call of Mother

After Padmapada's departure, Acharya Shankar began to feel an emptiness within him. Padmapada was his very dear disciple and association with him was spiritual. Subsequently Shankar sits down in *padmasana* and becomes engrossed in meditation. After some time, he feels a sudden and intense desire to meet his mother. He feels as if his mother is calling him. He stands up as his mind is in an upheaval. He can feel that his mother is in some trouble. He remembers the promise he had made to his mother. He calls his disciples, gives the necessary instructions for operating the *ashram* and departs for Kerala. He reaches his birthplace, walking tirelessly day and night.

When he reaches home, he finds his mother waiting for him on her deathbed. A neighbour is seated next to her and his mother is groaning, "Shankar... my son...!"

Shankar rushes to touch his mother's feet, crying, "Mother, I have come."

From where does so much power come in that frail and feeble body that his mother pulls him and embraces him. This soulful union of mother and son is breathtaking.

Mother affectionately replies, "Son, now I feel healthy because you have arrived. Go and take a bath and I will arrange food for you."

Shankar lowers himself into the same River Purna which flows behind his house. The waves wash away his fatigue. When he returns home, fresh food prepared by his mother awaits him.

The mother, who had been lying helpless on her bed before his arrival, now appears filled with fresh energy that could put any youth to shame.

At the request of her son, the mother also takes food. After the meal, the mother and son sit outside in the courtyard. Mother wants to hear the story of her son who had been away for so many years. Where did he stay? Where did he live? How did he survive? Shankar narrates the entire story of his experiences and in returns inquires about his mother's situation in the past few years. Mother tells that as soon as Shankar had left, she was helped by her neighbours for some days because of her wealth, but with the passage of time, their sense of service had begun to dissipate. They forgot the promise they had made to serve the owner of the property till she was alive. "They considered my old age as a burden and waited for my death. The people in the village are dissatisfied because according to them, service is given only when something is given in exchange. Why should they serve in vain? Son, in this village, only a few people are sympathetic."

No one had imagined that this son, engaged in the service of his mother, was an extraordinary monk whose scholarly voice would be heard by innumerable people as the voice of God; who in the name of religion had churned the sea of unrighteousness to revolutionise the whole nation. Neighbours and close relatives, snooping at the news of his arrival, are filled with envy and are surprised on catching a glimpse of him. They had assumed that Shankar, who had become a recluse in childhood, would have been eaten by the animals in the forest or bitten by poisonous snakes and scorpions while sleeping in solitude, but here the case was reversed. The deer-cub has not only survived but had returned as a lion. Now he will surely claim the right to his property and take it away from us. Trapped in the earthly mirage, these creatures attack him initially, "Hey, how are you a monk? Do monks return home after renouncing the world? If after so many days of renunciation, you have not given up your love for your home, your mother, then it means that you are a hypocrite."

Shankar looks at them with pity. He does not even consider them worthy of being replied and so he keeps on administering to his mother. His unresponsive behaviour makes the attackers feel all the more angry and they decide to launch their next attack. Shankar's eyes become wet with tears as his mother consoles him. Shankar feels that his mother's body is warm as if burning with fever. He escorts her to her bed and taking cold water in a vessel, moistens a towel in it and applies it on her forehead. This reduces her fever a bit.

The mother continues to look at her son, forgetting her fever and pain. She is like a cow, sad at the separation from her little calf. She had experienced that sorrow every day for so many years continuously. Today, with the sudden appearance of her son, she feels as if she has received everything. The moonlight of happiness shines on her face which had been burnt in the sun of sorrows. She rains kisses on her son's forehead and hands. Her dearest son has returned home today. The sad and colourless brick walls of the house also seem to be smiling.

She stares at the glowing countenance of her son, who is engaged in lowering her temperature with a wet cloth. When he had left this house and become a monk, he was a mere teenager, but now he has returned home endowed with the power of penance. Adolescence has now been replaced by youthfulness of a man. Mother feels proud to see his bull-like, strong, robust body. His large eyes are filled with tenderness and modesty, and his broad forehead indicates an amazing talent. Within her heart, the mother compares the father and son. Yes, his father also looked handsome, she feels. "Son, there was no one to give me water," she complains, returning to the present.

On hearing this, Shankar's eyes fill with tears. He was a minor at the time of leaving his home, with no knowledge about the wily world. He had no idea of the practical difficulties that his mother would face in his absence. How the mother must have lived her life after suffering the immense grief of separating from her husband and son, he could now realise. Lives of eminent people who follow high ideals have always been thorny.

The mentality of human society is strange! Those who come forward for the country or society or for the help of mankind, they get into trouble and the wheel of time crushes them and moves forward. Their families and loved ones face economic and material crises. On the other hand, those who cleverly change their direction with the wheel of time enjoy seats of convenience. Their prosperity grows like compound interest. History sings praises of them.

The mother of the Acharya, who had wandered in the forests for public welfare, is suffering in old age at becoming helpless and unwell. The relatives take advantage of her property and neglect the real owner while the rest of the world watches as mute expectator! How is the welfare of this society possible? "I had gone out to remove the darkness from the world but the world created darkness in my own house. O creator! Look at this anomaly!"

While doing penance, he had learnt of sages and monks renouncing all pleasures and living on tuber roots or on alms. There were some who despite surviving on leaves from trees or grass were engaged in serious spiritual practice. He had also seen some ascetics who lived only on water or on air, even though their bodies had dried up to become skeletons. Some were absorbed in experiments of knowledge, some in experiments of science. Although the society would enjoy the benefits of their experiments, the care of these ascetics was taken only by their close family members.

Ever since Shankar had come to know of this practical side of life, he had started worrying about his mother. When the longing became intolerable, he rushed towards his mother. He remembered his promise which he had given to his mother when he had left his home. On meeting his mother, he begins to massage her feet and she in turn closes her eyes in peace. She holds the son's hand, gets up and says, "Son, my Shankar, it is time for me to leave. I am satisfied to see you. I was waiting for you and my life was stuck in you. Now I can take my last breath in peace.

"Don't trust any of your kinsmen. Perform my last rites with your own hands. If possible, keep these servants together. I have no desire left now." While speaking, her voice begins to tremble and her words falter. Looking at the worried face of Shankar, she closes her eyes forever. It is a beautiful death – calm, painless and perfect! There is a look of great satisfaction on her face.

Shankar looks at his mother's face. She looks so serene even in those moments of eternal sleep as if a flower has fallen from its branch. Such a painless death is granted only to *nirvikar yogis*. Even all the knowledge of the great Shankar cannot stop his tears from flowing. After all, she was his mother, whom he had sacrificed years ago at the altar of his duty. Today was her final ritual.

He sends a servant to collect firewood and himself starts preparing for the last rites. No one gives fire to the servant; rather they come to argue with Shankar, "Shankar, you are a monk, so you are forbidden to cremate. You go away as it does not become you."

"I know both my duty and my religion; you people did not behave properly with my mother when she was alive. Now don't quarrel at her funeral and attend to your duty."

"You are violating the religion of renunciation in the greed for wealth. We will not participate in your sin..." Saying this, the family members leave one by one. They do not listen to Shankar's pleadings. With a heavy heart, Shankar says, "Due to your non-cooperation, I am not able to go to the crematorium for my mother; so I will perform her last rites here in the house itself. But remember, from today onwards your homes shall become crematoriums."

Meanwhile the servant arrives with wood and Shankar lights the funeral pyre of his mother. He watches her being absorbed in the blazing flames with his moist eyes. He feels that today his last bond with the world is being consumed. With the liberation of his mother, he becomes supremely independent. Now he is ready to set out on his campaign with unprecedented energy. By converting his pain into medicine, he is ready to heal the wounds of the world.

Even after performing the last rites of his mother, he neither leaves his home nor his birthplace. He regularly bathes in the holy River Purna during the wee hours and spends hours on the banks, engrossed in his study and contemplation. After that, he would return to his deserted home, perform the daily *yajna*, light a lamp in the memory of his mother and make future plans with a calm mind. As days go by, people begin to visit him. The crowd of devotees and volunters from all over the country arrive due to which, the busy routine of Shringeri envelopes him also.

□

46

Views of Shankar

King Rajshekhar of Kerala is a person with good taste. He not only admires the unique talent of Acharya Shankar but also appreciates his sacrifice and penance. He himself has come to attend the mourning of Acharya. Even before his arrival, the royal staff had made arrangements in Kaladi.

The king is engaged in conversation with Acharya while the crowd outside is proud to behold the splendour of the royal soldiers standing guard. The king had been suppressing his desire to control the religious anarchy prevailing in Kerala since a long time. Today he speaks to Acharya in this regard, "Swamiji, it would be better if you were to frame a code of conduct to eradicate evil and check socio-religious arbitrariness."

The Acharya smiles, "Your opinion would be best. I will write a small religious code so that the public can understand what is religious and what is against religion!"

The king returns along with his army after paying his due regards. Acharya writes a guide, describing the laws on the basis of his memory and by following which one can lead a religious life.

The king and his legal experts are very pleased on reading this precise code of conduct in simple language. They name it *Shankar-Smriti*. The king calls a meeting of Brahmins and priests and places this book in front of them. There is grave opposition, some of which is borne out of envy while some are opposed because *Shankar-Smriti* would put a halt to the arbitrariness practiced by Brahmins. Having all the necessary policy guidelines in one book, the priests can no longer subjugate or mislead the general public in the name of scriptures. Some Brahmins get so agitated at this new code that they feel it is an attack on their supremacy. Brahmins are respected like living gods on the earth. They are ruled only by their *sanskars* and discretion.

A very influential Brahmin stands up and tells the assembly, "O king, the attack on the reputation of Brahmins through this new *Smriti* is a sin. We will leave your kingdom in protest against it."

Another speaker says in a loud voice, "O king, this is a conspiracy by royal might to suppress the power of a *guru*."

Many people start to yell in his support. King Rajshekhar's prime minister pacifies him with a gesture and says, "We have heard your side. You seem to have some confusion in your mind. Maharaj Rajashekhar respects all Brahmins as per the clan tradition. You are enjoying your privileges to the fullest in our state. The state has never obstructed or placed obstacles because it is Maharaja's policy to give full freedom to intellectuals to express themselves; even to condemn the king or the state, so that they can be fearless and impartial in presenting a healthy criticism of the merits and demerits of political affairs."

"The goal of *Shankar Smriti* is not to attack the freedom or superiority of Brahmins. It has been composed by a great Brahmin teacher for implementation by every section of the society. Whoever is leading a holy life according to the *Smriti* should support it with confidence. Your support is necessary to stop the distortions that have creeped in our public and religious lives."

Some more doubts are raised and their clarifications are given on behalf of the state. This satisfies the majority in support of the new code; those who are in opposition choose to debate with Acharya. But on being defeated by the knowledge and arguments put forth by Acharya in the debate, they also turn into followers of Acharya.

The provisions of *Shankar-Smriti* are implemented by the entire state of Kerala with the support of Brahmins. The society also accepts these, knowing that their welfare lies in their implementation. This increases the importance of Acharya.

Now Acharya begins to miss the *ashram* at Shringeri. He thinks of taking leave from Kerala. KIng Rajshekhar politely requests him to stay on as he does not wish to be deprived of the company of Acharya. Accepting his request, Acharya sends a message to Shringeri, ordering his chief disciples to come to Kerala.

The disciples embark on their journey immediately on receiving their *guru's* orders. Soon they arrive in Kerala and Shankar is very pleased and no less are the monks on receiving their *guru's* blessings. In the evening, a meeting of disciples is organised in the presence of King Rajshekhar where the king says very humbly, "O revered Acharya, a great ritual is needed to bind the land of India in a single thread and I plead that you go out to conquer with my military force. Defeat the petty views of the people with your scriptures. Wherever you feel the need for exercising control, my armed forces will obey your orders."

Acharya does not agree with this proposal and says, "O king, I appreciate your feelings of nationalism; elimination of petty opinions is also necessary. Establishment of Sanatan Dharma is the goal of my life but this is not possible with the help of armed forces.

"The establishment of religion is not possible through force or violence. Religion is not something to be imposed with the sword. How many opinions have succeeded by resorting to muscle power? As long as Buddhism spread through the power of thought, it had its primacy, but as soon as it chose the path of bloodshed, it got ruined. India has never preached religion by sword. The supremacy of weapons is momentary; you can by force conquer the bodies of men, not their hearts."

"Then, O great sage, please tellme by what method can the renaissance of the nation and the establishment of religion be brought about?"

"Dear king, in my view this is possible only by winning the hearts of the people with bright conduct and intensity of knowledge. Moral values are not established by words, discourses and books, but by the best conduct of the superiors. The ruling class, feudals, priests, businessmen, officers should be truthful, just, firm but humble in their conduct. This is enough for the rest of the people; they merely tend to imitate.

"Young monks, who are full of love for the nation and want to work for public welfare, will renovate the nation with their restraint and penance. To establish religion, there is no need for an army."

King Rajashekhar humbly agrees with Acharya's reasoning. Acharya assures him that his preparations for a national renaissance are going on since the past several years and now they would be started afresh in a new form and in a more organised and planned manner. At this, Rajshekhar is convinced and pleased.

The preparations for absolute victory continue for a week. It is decided that the main campaign would be led by Acharya himself. He would start the journey from the south and go to the Himalayas in the north, through the major cities in the east and west before reaching the frontiers. Along with this, the disciples of the Acharya would take the campaign to the rest of the cities and villages.

During the preparations for the journey, Acharya instils in the minds of his disciples that this journey is meant to add and not to break. He says that its purpose is coordination; not fragmentation.

The myriad flowers of local beliefs, folk deities, dialects and traditions has to be woven into a beautiful garland which would bring mental and spiritual unity in this vast land. Just as a skilled farmer, while preparing the field with hard work, destroys the garbage, uproots the weeds skilfully, similarly with the same patience one has to refine and eradicate the ills in public life.

This absolute victory campaign is launched at an auspicious time when his meritorious disciples are fully trained. In the campaign, a group of disciples always takes the lead, stays in the village temple and connects with the villagers by practicing cleanliness, *yajna*-worship, hymns and describing the benefits of performing scriptural rites. The disciples answer the questions raised, explain the methods to overcome the natural calamities, diseases and inform about the arrival of Acharya.

Villagers eagerly await the arrival of Acharya, who wants to erect temples as energy centres of society as hd been done in ancient India. He says, "The temple is not only a place of worship, but is a centre of education and communication, health and rituals. Therefore, it is necessary to restore and consecrate temples."

□

47

Meeting Padmapada

The public listens to every word that Padmapada utters; the energy of his thoughts is visible in villages and towns. Innumerable people come to join this movement and the monks move forward, blowing the conch before changing the route. In this journey, today it is the turn of a famous pilgrim of Kerala to launch the campaign. Acharya is relaxed after worshipping the deity and preaching to the gathered public. Padmapada arrives at this moment. Acharya is filled with happiness to see him, but Padmapada begins to sob while bowing to him. Everyone is bewildered as to what could have prompted Padmapada to weep like a child! When Acharya inquires, he narrates the incident of the damage of his book by fire. Acharya consoles him, "Don't be emotional, Padmapada. I remember your complete book ad verbatim. I will recite the whole book for you to write. Now wipe away your tears."

Padmapada wipes his tears and *guruji* places his hand on his head to shower blessings on him. He now feels good and becomes calm. *Guruji* gives a patient hearing to the account of his journey and explains to him the 'social awakening' movement.

Padmapada is filled with enthusiasm as he has been depressed at the plight, filth and deceit in temples and pilgrimage sites during his campaign. He feels relieved that his great *guru* is venturing out on a salvation mission in the country as per the need of the times. Padmapada also joins this 'victory vehicle'.

Acharya, in spite of his busy schedule, narrates the content of Padmapada's book to him and gets his book written through his magnificent memory. Due to this amazing grace of his *guru*, Padmapada is so grateful that doubts assailing his mind disappear forever.

□

48

Victorious Enterprise

Acharya's message of change reverberates in cities and villages and with the addition of local talents, devotees and spiritualists, its size and appeal increases manifold. People stand for hours, waiting to welcome this wonderful 'awakening' journey. The echo of the conch shell, the sound of drums and cymbals resonating with cheers to welcome Acharya, present a splendid sight. Devotees stop in procession from place to place to garland the monks. They offer confectionery, dry fruits, drinks, milk and luscious food to consume on their tedious journey.

Acharya is the centre of attraction as he is adorned like a full moon of the night sky. To catch a glimpse of him, people are ready to endure any amount of inconvenience caused by the crowd. The immense popularity and success are adding to Acharya's worries. Whenever he finds solitude, he broods on what would be the next step to adopt after the glorious procession. He knows that fame and public enthusiasm are fleeting. To remove the ills in the society, there is need for continuous treatment. What should be the system? How to bring it about? Spreading the message of religion among the disciples, providing constant guidance to the general public and healing the ailing system to rid it of its deformities are the subjects of continuous discussion. Acharya believes that efforts to solve perennial problems should also be permanent and institutionalised.

Some disciples suggest that *ashrams* should be established from place to place so that they can serve as centres of power and their finances should be the state's responsibility. But Acharya rejects the suggestion of seeking state aid. He is of the opinion that involvement of the state increases the hold of the state, due to which not only the power of the society, but also the power of religion weakens. The control of religion should be supreme. If it were to fall in the hands of the state, then who will show the right path to the state and the king? The state-reliant religious power is bound to become a slave of the state power.

In India, since times immemorial, Sanatan Dharma has been nourished by the faith of the common man. The state has never been its owner; rather it has been a follower. Therefore, even the repeated storms of foreign invasions could not break its willpower. If religion were to follow the rule of power, then its foundation begins to waver as soon as there is a change in the state power. He dislikes the idea of religious leaders living at the mercy of the state.

The devoted listeners, who are daily recipients of the rain of knowledge during the victory march of Acharya, listen spellbound to his melodious voice with a mesmerising feeling. The effect of his voice is so full and sweet that the listeners feel contentment, yet crave for more.

"Our great forefathers gave Brahmins the wealth of knowledge and wisdom, but deprived them of real wealth to the extent that they had to depend on alms received from others for their sustenance, so that at the height of their position and honour, they would not get intoxicated and arrogant. Even if they were given financial strength, then also arrogance of knowledge and the pride of glory would have made them like Ravana. Thus the ideal of living a poverty-stricken life was given to them. To ensure that they would not become arrogant when the society bows its head with reverence at their feet, they were kept dependent on alms and charity.

"Whoever has the power of wealth or muscle power or spiritual power, can become an uncontrolled exploiter and impose his conditions on the social world. That's why the merchants were given financial power but kept deprived of spiritual might."

The disciples are eager to hear such interesting commentaries of the Acharya, who also exposes the deep mystic subjects in simple and clear words with full devotion.

□

49

Five-Deity Worship

As he proceeds on the journey, Acharya and his disciples realise the fact that one of the results of liberality and freedom present in Sanatan Dharma is that in one part of the country, one God is dominant and in the other part the other God dominates. He discovers that the number of devotees of the five *avatars* is more and there is also a struggle for their mutual dominance. The five *avatars* of these gods are – Ganapati, Shiva, Shakti, Vishnu and Surya. In order to resolve the conflict between the Shaivas, Vaishnavas, Shaktas and Ganapatyas, Acharya orders the worship of these five deities, making it mandatory for all. This system soon becomes popular as it encourages co-existence and reduces the unrelenting struggle.

Trained priests from their *ashrams* make the worship of the five deities an essential part of their rituals. Due to the establishment of five deities in the houses, social peace and harmony prevails.

Acharya's 'victory journey' moves fast like a river in flood. In this flood, the trees of sectarianism, narrow-mindedness, estrangement and enmity get washed away like straw. A new syncretic society begins to breathe.

□

50

Sages' Kumbh

There are innumerable differences in opinion across the country, but the generosity and freedom of Sanatan Dharma becomes a poisonous gland in due course of time. In the forest of anarchy, every new plant turns arrogant of becoming a tree. The branches themselves become hostile to the tree. This sense of arrogance and anarchy endangers Sanatan Dharma. Every sect has its monks, warriors and arena. Above all, there is no system or control over them.

Acharya knows that if the nation and society are to be organised into one unit, then its large and effective manpower has to be given a system, a way of life and a discipline. He had been contemplating and analysing this matter for many years. Now it is time to declare and follow some practical decisions. He organises a massive religious *kumbh* (congregation) of sages. In this *kumbh*, unusual sects of monks, sages with and without clothes arrive.

In making arrangements for their accommodation and food, a trained team of celibates is engaged. After months of preparation, this huge event becomes possible. Monks and sages are cordially invited from every corner of India. All have set up their own tents and canopies. Some of them are so untouched by the world of senses that the sky serves as their tent and the earth as their bed.

The invitation to this mega event is received by monks of all faiths from all directions – north, south, east and west. The invitation is extended to the sages from the caves of the Himalayas in the north to the slopes of the Sahyadris in the west; from the worshippers of Kamakhya in the east to Kumari Anteep across the Vindhyas in the south.

The call of Acharya Shankar resonates. In response to his call, troupes of sages, monks, nagas in saffron, black, white, red, yellow robes march towards the spot. A magnificent stage has been set up in the main area. It's as high as three men. From that dais, Acharya's speech is heard by the community, "O flag-bearers of *dharma*, greetings! You are welcome. God is one and according to our faith and dedication, we worship Him in infinite forms.

"The great culture and tradition which had given us the message of *vasudaiva kutumbakam*, in that same holy land one finds serious discord among the clans and races which are plagued by mutual bloodshed and wars.

"The period of great emperors is over. Now we have to take the responsibility of preventing political and social fragmentation, else the people engaged in fulfilling their duties and responsibilities will have to sacrifice themselves on the altar of foreign invasions and influences.

"Our holy land has been protected against foreign rulers for centuries and so no one has dared to attack, but the future seems bleak because the land is no longer protected today. Our rulers are engaged in mutual conflicts, the common masses are engaged in their life struggles while the intellectuals are immersed in the luxury of their wisdom. Their good fortune has made the upper class self-satisfied and luxurious. Our holy land, like a ripe succulent fruit, is open to any invader to attack.

"Our generosity has now become anarchy, our wonderful ideological freedom is utter arbitrariness and our diversity has now become a terribly divisive disease. Knowledge and wisdom have become the prerogative of a few; our religion is now hypocritical and inert and our faith has turned into superstition. The *Vedas, Upanishads, Smritis* compiled by great sages and ascetics have been burdened by arbitrary interpretations to the extent that that their study is no longer a part of the daily routine of Brahmins and priests. How can then a common man comprehend it?

"I have witnessed during my travels across the nation that our great religion is dying; our pilgrimages are centres of filth and deceit. The ancient temples are sheltered by spider-webs and bats.

"What about the people? Even the best of the best are moving away from the path of knowledge and the path of devotion to adopt the highway of luxury. Our holy rivers are being polluted, forests are being destroyed and greed is becoming the leading trend. Feelings of kindness, compassion and benevolence are nowhere to be seen. Before this terrible calamity destroys us all, I call upon you to awaken the masses and perform your duty unitedly."

He pauses for a moment while speaking, wipes the sweat from his forehead with his towel, drinks some water from his wooden vessel, takes a deep breath to inhale fresh air in his lungs and starts again, "We can collectively check this great cataclysm together or be destroyed by living apart. Can you guide us on what to choose?"

The audience replies in unison, "You guide us; we are even ready to sacrifice our lives to protect the nation and our culture."

Acharya Shankar happily continues, "Excellencies, in order to organise the nation, all the sages and religious leaders have to be united first. You are everywhere in this vast nation – from deserted forests to inaccessible caves, from remote villages to developed cities. It's my humble request that wherever you are, you must become the watchdogs of culture in your area of influence, win the hearts of the people through your righteous conduct and cultivate them.

"There should be public reading and recitation of *Vedas and Puranas* in the place you belong to. Educate and organise the society through regular hymns, worship and debates."

The audience replies in one voice, "Sir, we accept your submission. Please proceed to tell us further."

Acharya continues, "I have discussed and advised all the

scholars to unite and organise all the sages into a sect. Human beings do not have the same nature; therefore, these sects will be divided into ten types of monks called *Puri, Giri, Bharati, Saraswati, Tirtha, Vana, Parvat, Sagar, Aranya* and *Ashram*. These groups will be collectively called *Dashnami Sampradaya*."

After this, he threw light on the rationale and methods adopted for these names in detail. The audience is astonished at the subtle and comprehensive approach of his action plan. It is a revolutionary effort to organise the unmanageable. The whole house adopts the new system with one vote. Some reasonable amendments are included in the proposed system. Voices of opposition are also raised, but they are weak and solitary.

Acharya Shankar proposes to recognise six major votes, which too are passed with enthusiasm. After this great religious conference, all the monks get together and filled with a new enthusiasm, decide on who would reach which village, city, mountain, forest, pilgrimage centre, seashore, temple, monastery and *ashram* across the country, carrying the victory flag of Vedic culture as a mark of the great awakening campaign in the nation.

Acharya, along with his disciples, prepares to embark on a long journey to give impetus to this campaign.

It takes almost seven days to get over the fatigue of the mega event. Today, being the eighth day, Acharya starts on the journey along with his disciples. He reaches the Shaivite pilgrimage centre called Madhyarjun nearly at sunset and pays a visit to the deity in the Shiva temple of Madhyarjun. This region is dominated by Brahmins. Acharya is welcomed and given food and the temple courtyard to rest on.

The next day, people start gathering from early morning at the temple doorstep to catch a glimpse of Acharya. On hearing the clamour of the crowd, the meditating Acharya comes out and people are thrilled to see his charming personality. Impressed with his demeanour, more and more people arrive to become followers of monism.

His further journey has to be postponed at the strong insistence of the people who want to hear him. After two days, people allow him to proceed further at his continuous request. This congregation of ascetics marches forward to Rameshwaram. On the way, Acharya's mind concentrates on Tula Bhawani's shrine. His squad reaches before Acharya to make the arrangements for his stay despite being advised not to do so because of the presence of many groups of Shaktas, like Veerachari, *Pashvachari*, *Vaamachari* and Kolachari.

In the name of *tantric* worship of their goddess, all they know is to drink liquor, eat meat and enjoy sex. Their acts seem strange and abominable. In their company the citizens of the area also become inclined to adopt these nefarious activities. The educated and cultured are saddened and disappointed at this fall. As soon as they receive information about Acharya's arrival, they begin to prepare for his welcome.

Acharya's warm welcome at Tula Bhawani shocks the Vamacharis. They get disillusioned to see the local community offer their support. They decide to confront Acharya as they are filled with hatred and animosity. They personally have no faith in Acharya. They want to drive him away by humiliating him in front of everyone. Indecency lies in both their language and behaviour. They move ahead to frighten and suppress Acharya through brute force, without realising that they are facing one who cannot be deterred. Their leader is at the forefront. His mouth reeks of liquor. As soon as he notices Acharya, the people gathered to welcome the monk, reluctantly turn aside to give way to him as he marches forward, mouthing expletives. His companions, who follow behind him, are seething with anger and are ready to launch their attack. The people present watch with horror writ on their faces, though the likely victim of the attack is far from worried.

In his childhood, as a monk, he had been a witness to terrifying wild animals, bandits and dozens of all such kinds in the dense and inaccessible forests. He has now grown into a handsome youth; his able body oozes of physical fitness. When the aggressor notices the monk's muscular arms, despite his intoxicated condition, he realises that the duel would not be one sided. Pointing towards the Acharya, he yells, "You are a wily hypocrite."

Acharya replies with a tender smile as if he has not heard anything. Annoyed at this, he starts screaming in a louder voice, "You are immersed in the unreal non-duality, like a *bandhyaputra*. When there is information on distinction even in the time of dissolution, then where does you monism come?" He gives many such arguments but in the end, he is forced to admit, "We are worshippers of Adi Shakti and you too should worship her or leave the place after seeking forgiveness. Do not spread confusion here with your imaginary arguments."

Acharya puts forth his argument in a calm, but firm and vigorous voice, "I and my disciples also worship the world's mother but your method is against that prescribed in the scriptures. Brahmins should not drink alcohol. The abominations practiced by you in the name of worshipping the goddess are not religious and do not suit the Brahmins. If you were to renounce this unfair practice, then only can welfare take place."

It is difficult to say whether it is the authority in Acharya's voice or the muscular strength of his well-formed, strong and trident-bearing disciples that the Brahmins leave peacefully. Some of them even atone for their sins and become Acharya's disciples.

The news of Acharya's moral victory over the sensuous devotees spreads like wild fire.

After Tula Bhawani, the victorious group of young monks proceeds towards its next destination. While treading the path, the group begins to feel uncomfortable in the humidity present in the air. They realise that they are nearing the beach of Rameshwaram. Pilgrims from all over the country used to visit Rameshwaram to worship Lord Shiva. Even now a good number of pilgrims are present.

The name of Shankar has been heard by many and they are keen to meet him. The fact that they happen to be there at the time of his visit, they are not prepared to let this opportunity go waste. Shankar also likes Rameshwaram as he feels very energetic here.

Every day he would spend in worship of Shiva, interact with the people and provide guidance to the pilgrims. The Shaivites take inspiration from him to worship the five deities and adopt the ritual of *yajna*. Acharya stays a little longer here as he enjoys the sunrise and sunset in the sea of Rameshwaram. The recognition of Rameshwaram as a major pilgrimage site dates back to the time of Lord Ram.

Every day countless pilgrims arrive from all over India and enjoy hearing the spiritual discourse of Acharya, who feels very satisfied at this and is not anxious to leave soon. The local Shaivites take full advantage of his pious company.

After leaving Rameshwaram, this team of monks visits and upgrades many pilgrim centres to reach Srirangam. This is the stronghold of the Vaishnavas, who are upset to receive the information of Shankar's arrival. Their chief is worried as to why this Shaiva saint is coming amidst the Vaishnavas when he is considered to be an incarnation of Shiva? They become alert and wait to confront him.

When they receive the news that Acharya along with his thousands of disciples carrying tridents, is moving fast towards Srirangam, a panic assails the Vaishnavas. They fear an attack from the visitors. So the six types of Vaishnavas present (Bhakta, Bhagavata, Vaishnava, Pancha Raga, Vaikhanasa and Karmahi) unite in anticipation of imminent danger and start preparing for war against the arriving enemy.

When Acharya's forward squad sends this piece of news, Acharya asks them to meet the Vaishnavas and convey the message that he is not coming to wage war but to engage in debate, though the main aim is to pray to the idol of eternal Lord Vishnu. This plan works. When Acharya Shankar and his followers reach Srirangam, they are welcomed, not by swords, but by flower garlands. Accepting the welcome, Acharya enters the temple first to pay a devotional visit to Lord Vishnu. He outpours lyrical praise in his melodious voice.

The rise and fall of his voice mesmerises all those who are present, especially the priests. All get lost in the music of his notes. After the prayers, all recover from their state of trance to return to the cosmic world. His devotion and dedication remove every apprehension and hatred of the Vaishnavas. Now there is a rush in the number of Vaishnavaites who throng the temple. They are enchanted to find an amiable Shaivite among them. Acharya answers their queries and the Vaishnavites presume that probably Acharya realises the futility of Shaivism and is wanting to adopt the Vaishnava faith and that is why he is doing such Vishnu *bhakti* (worship). But when they hear Acharya offering prayer to Lord Shiva, their beliefs disappear. The distraught Vaishnavas inspire Acharya for a debate. When the Vaishnava leader invites him for a debate, Acharya readily accepts the offer.

The debate begins in the presence of prominent Vaishnava leaders at the appointed time. After the initial announcements and formalities, the Vaishnava leader announces, "I am the supreme Vaishnava, who holds the *mundadi* (the conch shell) and similar signs used by devotees of Lord Vishnu. That's why I will go to Vaikunth (abode of Lord Vishnu) after being freed from the ocean of *bhava* (the physical world). I wear Puranic signs; why don't you also wear these insignias?"

Acharya asks in a calm voice, "But is there any proof in the *Vedas* in this matter? It is written in the *Vedas* that the cause of salvation lies in the knowledge of Brahm (the Supreme). Rigorous penance for getting rid of one's sins and worship of God for purification of mind are the laws incorporated in the *Vedas*.

"The knowledge of distinction gets removed gradually by thinking that I am Brahm and the soul attains the Shiva element. It is written in *Shiv Gita* that 'I am Shiva.' With this feeling, the soul attains the Shiva element. Thus, you also can purify your mind by worshipping the five deities. Eliminate sins by performing the five great *yajnas* and try to attain the Vishnu element by drowning in the feeling that you are a part of Vishnu."

The Vaishnavite devotees are satisfied on hearing such an unbiased and relevant argument of the Acharya. Traditionally, he was initiated as the disciple of Acharya; now he tries to bridge the deep gulf between the Shaivites and the Vaishnavites. Many Vaishnavites also become his followers.

One day, after the discourse, a Vaishnava devotee asks him, " Swamiji, it is known to us that you preach worship of Ganesha, Shiva, Durga, Narayan and Surya, the five gods, but what is the justification for doing so? Please tell us about the *panch yajna*."

Swamiji replies in a humble voice, "Since time immemorial, the five gods have been worshipped in Sanatan Dharma. A person is free to choose any one of these deities as his favourite one, while the remaining four continue to assist the main deity. Unfortunately, when the devotees request their main deity by showing contempt for other gods, then differences in opinion arise. I have revived the ancient tradition of worshipping the five gods to unite the entire Sanatan Dharma in one thread and destroy every kind of narrow-mindedness.

"Brahma is one; you can worship Him in any form. He is one – Shiva, Shakti, Vishnu, etc. are all forms of the same *nirguna* (formless) Brahma. It is foolishness and ignorance for the worshipers to fight among themselves."

"Okay sir, we have understood. Now tell us about the five *yajnas*. It will be a great blessing."

Acharya replies in a patient and serious voice, "First is *Brahma yajna* with Vedic recitation and study, second *pitrayajna* through *tarpan,* etc., third is *homa* to create a charged field, the fourth is sacrifice – *bhutashuddhi* – by feeding the cows and birds, etc. and fifth is *nriyajna* which means hospitality shown to every guest. These five sacrifices are essential."

"But Swamiji, what is the need to perform so many sacrifices? If we sit for *yajna* all through the day, then how will the life of any householder go on?"

"Knowingly or unknowingly, man resorts to a lot of violence – mental, verbal and physical. These five sacrifices are essential to destroy the sin generated by all such forms of violence. This gives us an opportunity to check us from commiting sinful deeds and become free through atonement for the sinful deeds committed. Even after earning your livelihood, if you do not waste time over futile activities and addiction, then these five great sacrifices become easy to perform." Saying this, Acharya resolves the doubts in the questioner's mind.

Every day Vaishnavites arrive with new questions and every day Acharya tries to provide the relevant answers. Distances get erased through constant dialogue. Due to the efforts of Acharya, not only Shavites and Vaishnavites, but worshippers of Sun, Ganapati and Kartikeya draw close to each other. The disparate society begins to reunite.

Acharya is a tireless traveller. His team marches on a continuous journey. He is going to reach Kanchi within the next two to three days.

Kanchi is an ancient pilgrimage site. With the arrival of Acharya, there is great enthusiasm among the Shaivites and Vaishnavites of Kanchi. The preparations for his reception become a celebration in themselves. Maharaj Nandi Varman, the Pallava ruler of Kanchi, is also engaged since morning in preparations to welcome Acharya. Today this group of Sanatan travellers is reaching Kanchipuram. The routes are decorated with festoons, garlands and flowers. There is a sort of competition to be the first to host in both the parts of Kanchi – Shiva Kanchi and Vishnu Kanchi.

As soon as the pilgrims enter the borders of Kanchi, they are greeted with flowers and cheers. It is a grand welcome comprising the sound of conch shells, the trumpet of royal elephants and drums beats. It is felt as if a conquering emperor is being welcomed.

The king of Kanchi washes the feet of the pilgrims with fresh water and honours them by offering coconut fruit and garments to wear.

As is customary, Acharya first visits the deities. He prays to Shiva Kanchi. He is grieved to see that the temple in which Lord Shiva is worshipped in the *linga* form, by the name of Amresh, lies in a dilapidated condition. He performs the Rudra *abhishek* with reverence. He senses that there is no culture of regular prayer and worship here. From here he visits the Vishnu Kanchi on seeing which his grief doubles to find its state even more pathetic and neglected. He prays to Lord Vishnu, who is revered here by the name of Vardaraj.

Under his inspiration, the local Shaivites and Vaishnavites contribute to the reconstruction and restoration of these temples. The nearby rulers, including the king of Kanchi, give these temples state protection on the wishes of the Acharya. As a result, this ancient pilgrimage again blossoms on regaining its ancient prestige.

The eyes of the idol of Goddess Meenakshi, in the Meenakshi temple of Kanchipuram, seem so energised that an ordinary man is unable to gaze at them continuously with his eyes. Acharya attracts the entire energy of the Devi in a *yantra* and consecrates it. He expresses the desire to construct a temple over it. The king of Kanchi promptly orders the construction of the temple in a bid to fulfil the wishes of Acharya. The sky resonates with cheers for Acharya.

Acharya proceeds after bidding farewell to the king and the people of Kanchi. People beg him to prolong his stay but he knows that this is only a temporary halt, not the goal. He responds to people's love with twice more love and hatred with four times more love. By now his disciples too have understood that the answer to hatred is not hatred or enmity to enmity. Often they have noticed many people resorting to rude and barbaric behaviour but soon showing a change in their behaviour on witnessing the loving expression on Acharya's face, so much so that many are forced to become his followers.

□

51

War with Kapalikas

Acharya propagates non-violence and peace but is a worshipper of energy; not of weakness and mercy. His non-violence is non-violence of the mighty; it's not borne of compulsion. He keeps his disciples conscious of physical fitness. He is a skilled wrestler and sword-fencer. In his group, most of the Shaivites walk with a trident, so forest bandits and robbers avoid coming in the way of their journey.

Acharya along with his disciples visits Ujjain via Tamraparni, Venkatachal and Vidarbha. Maharaj Sudhanwa is eager to welcome him but there are lines of concern on his face. The community of Kapalikas is very active in his kingdom. The Kapalikas consider Acharya as an enemy. King Sudhanwa himself faces threats to his life from the Kapalikas. Krakach is the chief of the Kapalikas. He and his associates, being Brahmins, do not consider anyone else worthy of their attention. They are angry at the fame earned by Acharya's principle of monism because their method of spiritual practice is based on animalistic rituals. They worship their deity by savouring meat, drinking liquor and indulging in sex. The common people dread their malpractices.

Acharya's religious practice exposes the adultery that the Kapalikas indulge in. So their sole desire is to attack him and destroy his reputation to dust. Kapalikas weave a deadly plot against Acharya. On receiving this information from his spy, King Sudhanwa sends an excellent army for retribution.

The frantic and angry Kapalikas under the leadership of

Krakach surround the team of Acharya Shankar. He moves forward, using abusive words and raises his dagger to kill Acharya, but the latter remains unmoved. All the more angered at his calmness and fearlessness, Krakach, before landing his dagger on Acharya, is killed by a mighty Naga monk's trident. A fountain of red blood spurts out, drenching both his body and that of the Naga monk. A fierce battle ensues between the Kapalikas and Nagas. The army sent by King Sudhanwa brings the battle to a decisive end. The violent Kapalikas, for the first time, experience the taste of defeat. They did fight valiantly, but are defeated. Their chief warriors get killed. Whoever looks at Acharya's still posture amidst the blood-soaked battlefield and groans of the wounded is reminded of Lord Krishna in the battle of Mahabharata.

The Naga *sadhus* show amazing fighting skill. They fight intelligently and none of their warriors get killed, though some are injured.

King Sudhanva makes proper arrangements for treatment of the injured and for respectful cremation of the dead. The surviving Kapalikas surrender to the king's army. The dominance of the Kapalikas comes to an end forever. At the request of Acharya, the Kapalikas are pardoned and freed. Most of them turn to self-purification through atonement and are initiated as disciples of Acharya. Now they leave adultery and take to the practice of evening prayers, worship of five deities and performance of five *yajnas*. There is soon a re-establishment of Vedic religion.

Acharya, an idol of compassion, along with his disciples, now moves forward. At every step, some obstacle or difficulty awaits him. In the fertile land of India, the differences in opinion continue to sway – at some places it is the Charvak followers, at others it is the Kshapanaks and at still others are the atheists. Cultivating them through compassion and persuasion, the pilgrims enter Andra Pradesh.

□

52

At Jagannath Puri

After re-establishing the Vedic religion in Andhra, Acharya reaches the famous pilgrimage centre of Jagannath Puri of Kalinga. He enters the temple to offer his prayers and is surprised and sad to find the idol of Shri Jagannath missing. He notices the head priest worshipping the Saligram rock in the form of Lord Jagannath. This prods him to enquire, "O learned scholar, where is the idol of Lord Jagannath?"

At first the priest ignores him but when Acharya persists, the priest takes him to a secluded corner and says in a voice steeped with sorrow, "Swamiji, to protect the wooden deity of Lord Jagannath at the time of foreign invasion, the priest shifted the idol to a jewel box and buried it at some place near Chilkahad. The foreign invaders killed all the prominent persons but could not lay their hands on the deity or the jewel box. The location of the jewel box is unknown; therefore Saligram is worshipped instead."

Acharya becomes distraught to learn about the sacrifice made by the priests. He praises these virtuous persons in his heart and wonders if the generations to come would ever get to learn of the sacrifice made by the temple warriors in the past? He returns to the present when he hears, "Swamiji, we have heard of your name a lot. You have come here only by the grace of Lord Jagannath, so please guide us in recovering the precious idol."

Acharya consoles him and asks, "If the jewel box is found again, will you be prepared to re-consecrate the deity of Lord Jagannath?"

The priests happily consents. Acharya immediately gets absorbed in meditation while the priests wait excitedly to receive the good news. The servants of the temple also bring the equipments like spade, shovel, etc. for carrying out the excavation work. However, Acharya continues to meditate while the priests await impatiently yet reverently for the meditation to get over. After several hours, there is movement in the meditating body. Acharya says, "Under a huge banyan tree on the eastern side of Chilkahad and in the northern part lies the jewel box. Go there and dig it out."

The priests burst into joyous applause on hearing this statement of Acharya. They reach the designated site and begin to dig. Their gratitude and happiness know no bounds when they locate the jewel box.

The jewel box is ceremonially carried to Acharya who is in the temple. In the midst of Vedic chants and at the auspicious hour, the wooden deity of Lord Jagannath is consecrated. Acharya makes arrangements for scripture-based worship to be performed with the participation of the local people of Puri and the king of Kalinga.

Acharya visits the beach of Puri and feels the need for spreading the message of Sanatan Dharma to keep the religion alive and active; otherwise the jewel box of religion would get lost again in the waves of history. The people of Puri repose their full faith in Acharya and do not want him to leave. But Acharya desires to move on like the flowing water so that the weeds of distortions are eradicated and the Sanatan truth is re-established. He has less time but more work and doesn't want to waste even a single moment. His disciples visualise him as not only a *dharmayogi* but more as a *karmayogi*, who never gets exhausted, never stops but lives by chanting the *mantra* of '*Charaiveti, charaiveti*' day and night.

After handing over the arrangements at Jagannath temple to the residents of Puri, he departs. His next destination is ancient Magadha.

□

53

Devotees of Yama

The energetic disciples under the leadership of their Acharya start moving towards Magadha. At a place near Yamasthapur, they halt to take rest. There is a curiosity among the disciples regarding the name 'Yamasthapur'. They wonder at the name given to this place. They ask among themselves, 'Does Yama live here or is it his birthplace?" When the curiosity fails to subside, they turn to their *guru* to enquire. The pleased Acharya replies humorously, "Most of the people here worship the God of Death as He is their adored God, hence the name Yamasthapur. Go and take rest and seek your clarifications on reaching the place."

After the noon hours, the evening makes its presence felt. The Sun-god begins to gather his rays in the distant horizon while the group of young ascetics reach Yamasthapur.

They are astonished to see the grand temple of the God of Death. The faith of the people who worship Yama is so deep that they too wear the clothes of Yama and get the picture of the buffalo inscribed on their strong arms. They wear a horned crown and a black mark on their heads.

The local progenitors welcome Acharya and his team. The locals look at them with curiosity. After dinner, everyone rests. Next morning, when Acharya goes for his daily worship ritual, he finds the Yama-worshippers waiting for him. Acharya offers them a place to sit and the disciples welcome them with fresh water. The chief of these unusual worshippers of the God of Death begin to speak, "O great preacher, we have heard stories of your miracles, but we are the worshippers of Yama, who is our beloved God and is the master of creation, maintenance and destruction. He alone is Supreme. Brahma, Vishnu, Mahesh all emerge from Him. Therefore, discard your views and worship Yama, the Lord of All and your welfare will take place."

Having said this, he looks triumphantly at the brightly lit faces of Acharya and his disciples. He is disappointed to find that his powerful presentation has had no effect on them.

Acharya replies with a mild smile, "I find your view against the *Vedas, Puranas, Smritis* unacceptable. Undoubtedly Yama is an important and prominent deity. His worship is religion-oriented just as faith in other gods and goddesses is a matter of personal interest. But we will have to look at the facts in the discussion of religion and only then will we be able to find the truth. The fact is that the *Kathopanishad* says that Yama is not Brahma. *Markandya Purana* tells that the benevolent Mahadev saved one of his devotees from Yama and tortured Yama. Worship of Yama can be helpful in purification of mind, but salvation is attained only by knowledge of Brahma; not by worshipping deities."

Acharya's logic wins over the Yama worshippers as well. His calm exterior and adorable speech has a magic effect on them and they become his disciples. For the next one month, during Acharya's stay, they continue to gain knowledge by visiting his camp and by the time of Acharya's departure, they have been initiated into the monistic path of *manasa, vacha* and *karmana*.

Acharya does not force them to relinquish their faith in Yama; instead he balances it, as has been his way throughout. He has come out to add, not to break. He does not impose the truth, but illumines it. The rest of the work gets done automatically.

□

54

Again Prayag, Again Varanasi!

After leaving Yamasthipur and moving towards Prayag, memories of the past begin to trouble the mind of Acharya. He remembers how twelve years ago, he had come to Prayag with the desire to debate with the great Kumaril and got entangled in the fabric of dramatic events that happened one after another till he left for Mahishmati, on the advice of Kumaril.

He vividly recalls the last moments of the great Kumaril and it seems as if everything has just happened! He pays homage to Kumaril within his heart as his story of self-sacrifice has inspired many young minds to protect religion and culture. For most of Shankar's disciples, Kumaril has become an ideal hero who gave up his life with a smile. He really rules the young hearts.

Acharya regularly narrates inspiring stories before going to rest to hisdisciples and the common people. Today he has thought of narrating the story of Kumaril. In tonight's halt, when he narrates the story of the great Kumaril's struggle and self-sacrifice in response to the foolish attempts to crush Sanatan Dharma through autocracy of Buddhism, the listeners get shocked. It seems as if Kumaril has been revived and the night passes while discussing his bravery. In the morning, during the wee hours, this group of religious warriors proceeds towards Prayag.

After reaching Triveni Sangam, everyone bows down in reverence and choses a place of rest near the Sangam. Prayag is one of the holiest cities and very popular as a pilgrimage site. It hs been called a *tirtharaj* (the king of pilgrimages). Since ancient times, the *triveni* of religion, learning and culture flows here. Innumerable people do *kalpavas* (by meditating, a person becomes new in mind and body) at Triveni Sangam with the desire for liberation. Here the crowd of visitors and devotees never lessens. In every sixth year, Ardha Kumbh and in the twelfth year full Kumbh fairs are organised, in which the stalwarts of religion arrive with their disciples to sermonise on religion. Challenging the ice-cold weather of the month of *Magh* (December-January), thousands of devotees perform religious rituals.

Throughout the year, on every full moon and every new moon day, devotees from every corner of the country come to take the holy bath. Thus, in Prayagraj, religious programmes go on day and night. The arrival of religious saints and sages is a regular affair at Prayag, but the arrival of Acharya Shankar is an exceptional occasion for the people of Prayag because they still remember the monk who communicated with the great Kumaril and made him his disciple. Who can remain without seeing the frequently talked-about divine monk who had cast a lasting impression on the minds of those who had seen him with his wonderful personality, profound knowledge and self-effacing attitude?

The local residents of Prayag have begun to gather to choose a select spot for seeing the Acharya. Acharya, after retiring from his everyday spiritual practice, pacifies the thirst for knowledge of these visitors. In these religiously-thirsty devotees of Prayag, there are followers of all faiths. Some are worshippers of natural elements, like the wind, some of fire and some of the sun or Mahalakshmi, Vishnu, Shiva or Ganapati who are no less worshipped. Apart from this, the believers of many philosophies are also active here. Their different beliefs have been initiated by sage-like persons who were genius in their own time and the common man found salvation through them. Thus, they come with unwavering faith yet long to hear the Acharya too.

With the arrival of Acharya, the stalwarts of different faiths start to gather to seek the possibilities of debate. The generous

Acharya warmly welcomes all these devout warriors. By voicing their opinion, not only do the adversaries underline the superiority of their opinions, but also reveal the secrets of their inner *sutras*. This way both the listener and the speaker feel blessed. Acharya does not hesitate to voice his views or point out the shortcomings that have crept in due to the delusions of devotees of special sects.

His fair, impeccable personality and kind demeanour overshadow the differences in opinion. All the warriors of religion return after discovering the ultimate truth that different beliefs are like different paths, which ultimately lead to the same God. The warriors of religion who are still desirous of debate are given the opportunity to be defeated in the debate.

Every day the people of Prayag see people crushed under the divine talent of Acharya and gradually turn into his disciples. Three months pass in the blink of an eye. Having achieved complete triumph over both the hearts and minds of the people of Prayag, Acharya, the idol of joy, now treks towards Benaras. Thousands of *ashrams* made of grass-thatched roof at Triveni Sangam lie deserted after his departure.

The people of Prayag do not want to bid him farewell, but who knows more than them that the running water and the sparsely clothed *yogi* cannot be kept tied to one place.

□

55

Vishwanath in Kashi

Arrangements have been given the final touch to welcome Acharya at Kashi, but it takes Acharya and his team seven days to cover the distance between Prayag and Kashi. In the villages and cities falling on the way, the crowds do not permit the pilgrims to move ahead without being welcomed. The reception gates are embellished with mango blossoms and banana leaves. The village damsels keep dancing and singing auspicious songs. The place where he stops, sees huge crowds of devotees waiting for him for several hours with garlands and dry coconut fruits on both sides of the road.

Men, women and children, both old and young, are eager to have a look at him. Brides shower whole-grain rice, sandalwood powder and flowers from their homes as he passes on the streets below. Devotees are anxious to touch his feet and despite his steady refusal, it has no effect on them. People don't pay heed without taking the soil of his feet. Every village and city is eager to hear the preachings on *dharma* from the divine mouth of Acharya. He utilises these opportunities to attack the evils, laziness and despair. His ideas seem revolutionary to the masses as he tries to de-root social evils, distinctions of high and low, untouchability, witch-craft and alcohol consumption. His social reform programme with the *mantra* of monism becomes very popular among the youth, women and men. He gives the *mantra* of unity to the entire society and which is elimination of mutual enemity in religious beliefs.

Even the tireless journey for seven days and nights does not lessen his cheerfulness and enthusiasm. Acharya seems to be full of a new energy every time he meets new people.

A grand reception is being organised at the doorway of ancient Kashi, but the heart of Acharya is anxious to see Lord Vishwanath. After attending the reception, he quickly reaches the Vishwanath temple and gets overwhelmed and deeply absorbed in worship. His heart fills with divinity and his energy seems to emanate and spread all around. It is an inspiring sight for the visitors. Acharya Shankar, who is considered to be an incarnation of Lord Shiva, is immersed in the worship of Lord Shiva. This spectacle makes the devotees feel blessed.

After worshipping Vishwanath, Acharya leaves for the ancient Manikarnika shrine where he is expected to rest. According to the legend, Manikarnika *tirtha* has a holy tank made of *sudarshan chakra* of Lord Vishnu. The name of this place was famous as Manikarnika due to the various gems and ornaments that fell from the ears of Lord Shiva. This place is specially dear to Acharya because it is related to the unbreakable bond between Lord Vishnu and Lord Shiva. Twelve years ago, when Acharya had come to Kashi as a child monk, then also he had stayed here; now also he enjoys taking rest in Manikarnika shrine.

After reaching Manikarnika, Acharya goes to rest, but where is rest for Kashi? Kashi is a city of hyperactivity under the umbrella of Baba Vishwanath. Even when Baba Vishwanath sleeps after the *shayan aarti*, the arrival and departure of pilgrims continues on various routes leading to Kashi. Vishwanath may blink his eyelids even for a moment but Kashi, busy in welcoming and wishing farewell to its devotees, does not have this amenity. Kashi is the city of scholars, great scholars and greater scholars. Whoever comes here is put to the test. There is a Kashi Scholarly Council to tighten the scholars; to tighten the *dharmacharyas* is a Dharma Council; to tighten the rest, the bulls and ladders of Kashi.

Devotees are overwhelmed and may remain so, but the abbots of religion are not enchanted by this young South Indian saint. They are waiting to defeat him in debate and moreover this is not Prayag; it is Kashi. It is not a city of pure devotion, yet the sincerity of knowledge is needed, and Acharya Shankar is not the first *tirthankar* (a saviour who makes a path for others to follow) to visit Kashi! *Tirthankaras*, spirituals and religious leaders have been coming here in all ages, but the city of Baba Vishwanath does not let anyone else sit on its head. Even Gautam Buddha had to establish outside Benaras, at Sarnath; then how long can this delicate youth stay in front of the abbots of Kashi?

Such conversation is common in the lanes leading from the Vishwanath temple to the long, wide banks of River Ganga. The sagacity of the people of Kashi cannot be underestimated, whether one sifts cannabis, rubs tobacco leaves or spins yarn. A confectioner frying *jalebi* in hot oil is equipped with the knowledge of burning wood in the furnace as also the *Kathopanishad*. Kashi has made up its mind to be a witness to a new intellectual duel.

Monks or bulls – who are in majority at Kashi? It is difficult to say. It is said that there are as many sects as there are human beings in Kashi – Shaivas, Shaktas, Vaishnavas are everywhere, so why would they not be in Kashi? Moon and Mars, along with the worshippers of the *guru*, the priests of Siddha, Gandharva and Vetal can be seen here. Apart from the *hathayogi*, *rajyogi*, atheists, *charvakwadi* (worldly ones) are also seated here. How can it surprise one to have the worshippers of Saraswati and Mahalakshmi sitting together in this city of knowledge and prosperity? How can the gathering of scholars of so many hues and colours refrain from plunging into the intellectual struggle?

So they leap one by one into the intellectual arena and return defeated and humiliated. Those who suffer from the disease of conceit get cured with a single dose of monism given by Acharya. Those who suffer from indigestion of knowledge, they start feeling healthy at the mild smile of Acharya. Those who do not even believe in God begin to see Acharya as God. All in all, the more severe the disease, the fastest is the cure. In a few days, there is no scholar left in Kashi who has not gained knowledge by entering the intellectual arena. In the end, the differences of opinion in Kashi remain the same but the dust of confusion and discrimination gets wiped away by Acharya. This is his method of treatment.

Not only the general public, but a group of specific disciples, who suffer from desires and longings of this world, come forward to place their doubts in front of the Acharya. "*Guruji*, looking at the petty desires of worldly householders and the gluttony of royal men, it seems that we are banging our heads on a hard rock. You have come to distribute the nectar of monism, but they are not thirsty for it. You offer the *mantra* for national unity but their interest lies in controversies and conflicts. Under such circumstances our campaign will prove ineffective."

Acharya patiently hears and smiles. He observes that most of the disciples agree with the speaker, so he says, "Yes, we are engaged in a difficult mission. The residents of our great nation are busy in the struggles of life in which the maintenance of family is their goal. Those who have risen above the level of maintenance are engaged in the accumulation of wealth. This task, though intricate, is not impossible. When you start getting discouraged while hitting the inert rock of the society, then remember those water streams which constantly leak water to leave their marks on the rocks.

"If even a mild stream of water can pierce a stone, then we have no reason to despair in awakening the minds of living human beings. Son, to leave innumerable people in the darkness of ignorance, in the quagmire of illiteracy, in the hell of poverty to let them burn bit by bit is a serious crime.

"My children, as the Sun-god has been continuously illuminating the world since times immemorial and without getting tired, without despair, so should we be constantly engaged in the salvation of our great Vedic culture. That is why our ancient sages have given the formula of '*Charaivati, charaivati*'."

The disciples' confidence returns. They get satisfied and the darkness of despair dissipates through the great logic hidden in the soft voice of the Acharya.

□

56

Bhaj Govindam *Mooda Mate*

On the way, while going to the temple of Kashi Vishwanath, Acharya hears a *pandit* recite loudly and learn grammar while seated on a platform. His eyes turn towards his face. He notices that the Brahmin's face has turned red on reciting the rules of grammar in his full-throated voice and he begins to sweat. His mind and life are engrossed in cramming the grammar. On seeing Acharya halt, even the disciples stop and begin to stare at that Brahmin.

Shankar gpes to him and keeping his wooden staff and water vessel on the ground, says affectionately, "Son, grammar is a means, not an end. Child, don't waste your time in learning by heart the basic rules of grammar. Remember Govinda and chant Govinda's name. When death arrives, grammar will not protect you." Saying this, the poet in his heart awakens and he recites a beautiful poem:

Bhaj Govindam, bhaj Govindam,
Bhaj Govindam mooda mate.

The audience is overcome with emotions on hearing the confluence of Acharya's tone, rhythm and emotion. The Brahmin stops learning his grammar and joins his disciples.

□

57

Hail Ujjayini

The devotees of Saurashtra have come to Kashi to plead with Acharya to visit their Saurashtra. Acharya accepts their invitation now that his mission to restore the glory of monism in Varanasi and coordinate the different opinions has been accomplished. So, he departs for Saurashtra with his illustrious disciples.

As always, this expedition is useful in awakening the people and bringing the society together. Wherever this fascinating group of young ascetics goes, the local scholars join in, but the number of pilgrims does not exceed a limit because Acharya and his disciples initiate new people they meet on their journey into managing the local religious places at the next halt. Thus this religious journey is like a vibrant and dynamic training centre.

The process of establishing Sanskrit schools by motivating intelligent and wealthy people from place to place is also carried on side by side with the task of teaching Vedanta and the integration of society. In these schools newly initiated graduates are assigned the task of imparting knowledge about religion along with grammar, economics, etc.

The team now marches towards the ancient holy city of Ujjayini. Ujjayini is the land of Mahakal and the capital of the kingdom of Avanti. It has been a city of devotees, philosophers, poets, scientists and astrologers since ancient times. The king of Avanti is present in person at the main entrance of Ujjayini to receive Acharya. The learned councillors of the state and the citizens of Ujjayini, along with the royal elephants and horses, offer a warm welcome to Acharya. Ujjayini is a land of festivals, so at Acharya's arrival, the town wears a festive look. The trumpets blow and Ujjayini is embellished like a newly-wed maiden. Amidst the continuous rain of flowers, a group of happy people enter the Mahakal forest with Acharya. Here the royal employees persuade the masses to stay on. The disciples and the royal men accompany Acharya towards Mahakal because the huge crowd already gathered there has left no space for more devotees to come.

Acharya quickly enters the sky-kissing temple of Lord Mahakal with his disciples following behind. He is overwhelmed at the reverence shown in the presence of Mahakal. A lyrical melody erupts from his throat. He is imbued with the feeling of supreme bliss that has touched his heart and penetrated his soul. A sparkle of light engulfs his system and he becomes one with the Supreme Brahma.

After a few moments of meditation, he returns to the world. He notices some priests taking away the Mahakal's adornments with reverence for a bath with water. Amid Vedic chanting, the *shivalinga* is bathed with water, milk, curd, sugar, honey and *panchamrit*, etc. A young priest then adorns Mahakal very skilfully like a painter with the help of other priests. In a few moments a graceful and captivating *linga* emerges and it is decorated with fresh flowers.

Acharya beholds this magnificent form of Mahakal with half-open eyes and feels that nowhere can people find such a subtle example of the transience of the world! If the world understands this process of continuous adornment and wiping, then the futility of both sorrow and joy would be learned.

The priests complete the adornment with agility while musical instruments like bells, gongs, cymbals, etc. continue to be played. The decorated plate with lit lamps is in the hands of the chief priest as he is busy giving the final touches to the evening prayers to start. This grand event of music, chanting and prayer reaches its climax with the blowing of the conch. Acharya pays obeisance to Mahakal and after the flame in the lamp dies out, he and his disciples emerge from the sanctum.

There is an arrangement for leisure in the huge pavilion of the temple. The crowd of devotees and satisfied visitors have now gone. The full moon lights up the sky of Ujjayini. The temple premises bear a spiritual and sanctified look. Acharya enters the *yoganidra* as soon as he finds solitude and his co-travellers, tired after the long journey, fall asleep on their beds.

As the night ends, even before the birds wake up, the monks need to get up to worship God. So they take their bath and complete their routine activities. Due to a continuous practice of this routine, Acharya and his disciples feel pure. They are curious to observe the special worship of Mahakal, about which Acharya had often quelled their curiosity by saying that they would get to see it, on crossing Ujjaini.

Acharya and his disciples reach the sanctorum to attend the *bhasma arti* wherein the priest sprinkles ash on the adorned Mahakal. The fine particles of ash are sieved through the cloth so as to adorn Mahakal with it. The sound of bells, gongs and chants grow louder. Devotees watch the proceedings of this ritual from a big room outside the sanctorum. The idol of Bhootnath is seen covered in a cloud of fresh ash in the sanctorum. The chanting by the priest, who repeatedly sprinkles ash, reaches a crescendo and the entire sanctum gets engulfed in ash.

Acharya and his disciples are overwhelmed and bow down in deep devotion to Mahabhuta Mahakal. On returning from *bhasma arti*, Acharya summons Padmapada and asks him to invite Bhaskar *pandit*, the eminent scholar of Ujjayini, for a debate. Bhaskar Pandit had been waiting for this moment since the day he had received information of Acharya's arrival.

The debate starts in the huge pavilion of the Mahakaal courtyard at the appointed time. The people of Ujjayini, addicted to such serious debates, receive their intellectual gratification from such events. So, well before the appointed time, not just the pavilion, even the outer courtyard gets occupied. The love for poetry of the people of Ujjayini is so immense. The royal court has seen performances of best and better poets, leading litterateurs, playwrights, dancers, actors and clowns, who look forward to presenting their performance in front of the royal court. It is said that in India, whoever has a passion for reciting poetry, should never miss going to Ujjayini. The poet can recite his poem in the regular assembly of poets and poetic connoisseurs but if that assembly decides in his favour and declares him a poet, then he is declared a worthy poet, else his level is not more than a mere rhyme-composer.

In this emotionally-charged atmosphere at Ujjayini, a debate between Acharya, the rising sun of Sanatan Dharma and the scholarly Gaurav Bhaskar is being held. Who cannot be there? Which learned man or scholar will not be present? On the other hand, Acharya, whose sun of youthful talent shines with abundant energy as he is able to convince even reputed scholars like Mandan Mishra to become his disciples. He sets out on this victorious journey with great resolve. He has to preserve all the branches of Sanatan Dharma to save this divine culture from getting extinct. He considers this earth since infinite times as one composite family and sees the Supreme in all beings, reaching the ultimate state of spirituality through the *Vedas* and *Upanishads* and caring for the welfare of all.

His goal in Avanti cannot be accomplished without defeating Bhaskar *pandit* and making him his ally. The debate starts at the appointed time. Acharya propounds his theory of monism while Bhaskar *pandit* fires all the arrows from the quiver of his knowledge to refute it. But, despite a sincere effort, he is unable to resist defeat. By one vote the entire assembly declares Acharya as the winner. Acharya offers full respect to Bhaskar *pandit* for his arguments and intimately offers him a seat near himself.

Bhaskar *pandit* is filled with reverence for Acharya after

seeing his resolve and offers full cooperation in initiating more disciples for Acharya. As soon as the news spread in Ujjayini about the message of monism, the city residents gather in the meeting hall, not for the sake of debate, but out of their interest in Sanatan religion. Acharya's exposition enchants the listeners, while his melodious voice enamours the people of Ujjayini.

□

58

Saurashtra to Nation

Assimilating and surprising Ujjayini, Acharya departs for Saurashtra. On revisiting the pilgrimage centres of Girnar, Somnath, Prabhas, etc., he communicates and collects information while walking on the seashore to reach Dwarka.

He has left behind his fame in Avanti. Even after his departure, the impression of his intellectual acumen remains imprinted on the public mind for a long time. Avanti has been a fort for religious and Sanskrit scholars, but Acharya manages to defeat scholars like Vana, Mayur, Dandi, Bhaskar and the like. Many Buddhist and Jain religious scholars have taken refuge under Acharya in this battle of knowledge. Shaivites, Vaishnavites, Pashupati, Shakta – all have accepted the superiority of monism, as a result of which Avanti's interest in monism gains momentum. Avanti begins to tread on the footprints of Acharya.

But where is rest for Acharya? He is engrossed in quenching the heat of the route by drinking fresh water from the pious Gomati river, after accepting a warm welcome in Dwarka. Whenever and wherever he descends into a river, his childhood memories come alive. Every river reminds them of Kaladi's Purna river and momentarily every river becomes pure for him. The same thing has happened even today. He emerges from the river, wipes his body with a towel, changes clothes and climbs up to visit Dwarkadhish. He bows with reverence in front of the idol placed in the beautiful architectural structure of Dwarkadhish temple. Thousands of miles away from his birthplace, Lord Krishna of Vrindavan and

Mathura in this Gurjar country had become Dwarkadhish. The similarity in his and Acharya Shankar's life-story is that both are highly esteemed even outside their native land.

The residents of Dwarka are filled with enthusiasm on hearing of Acharya's arrival as there is a fair number of religious men and women keen to meet him. Dwarkapuri is dominated by the Pancharatra sect. They wear conch and *chakra* tattoos on their arms, *tulsi* leaves in their ears and marks on their forehead. Acharya's disciples look at them with curiosity and ask about them.

Acharya tells them that they represent subjects like the supreme principle, liberation, yoga and the world. Therefore, they are known as *pancharatra*, i.e. the followers of five-knowledge sect. Their principles are described under the Narayani *tantra* of *Mahabharata*. The chiefs of the *pancharatra* sect become disciples of the Acharya after facing defeat in a debate. Acharya leaves for the next halt after expressing his affection to them.

This team of tireless pilgrims hoists the flag of religion wherever it reaches, propagating the *mantra* of monism in Tushkar, Sindhudesh, Gandhara, Purushpur, etc. Acharya's journey is one of the greatest in human history. Wherever this huge religious army of hundreds of disciples, thousands of Brahmins and countless seekers go, hypocrisy, discrimination between high and low and mutual animosity get eradicated. Acharya's charming message makes the audience his followers. It is not in anyone's mind that this campaign of national integration will prove to be a great one; all that is known is that Acharya's vision is exceptional. He constantly works and wishes to make good use of each living moment, without forgetting that he does not have much time. His responsibilities are more. India is not just a country but a great country. The message of national awakening and integration, the campaign to uproot hypocrisy and unrighteousness in religion is so important that he cannot stay more than a single day at one place.

For so many months he is in a continuous journey and still a lot remains to be done in the darkness of ignorance and for that, he has to be constantly on the move!

They have moved from South India and are drawing near Kashmir in the north. By the time he reaches here, he has interviewed different people, learned different languages, met different sects that no one seems unfamiliar to him anymore. His disciples too have received a wide exposure to the diversity of India and come to realise that diversity is only a product of local circumstances. The differences are superficial due to diversity of language, dress, food and hymns but they are no hindrance to the unity of mankind. Diversity saves life from becoming dull. Acharya has taught his disciples and devotees to respect diversity. He has said that it is impossible to think of nationalism without the respect for local. He says that the sages who bow down to their village and personal deity do experience truth.

Kashmir is the main centre of Indian culture. The Goddess of Knowledge is worshipped here by the best scholars of India. Whatever is best in Sanskrit, culture, religion and spirituality is adorned here.

□

59

Omniscience in Kashmir

Srinagar is a historical city. 'Sri' means the 'city of prosperity', the land of art, culture, spirituality and beauty. It is a significant halt for Acharya's victorious march because here is present the famous temple of Saraswati, the Goddess of Learning and here is established the seat of omniscience. The right to the seat of omniscience is only to the one who is omniscient, that is, one who is absolute in the knowledge of all the scriptures. Along with it, one should be capable of understanding 'this' and the 'other' world and be accepted by the people for his wisdom and spiritualism. The best scholars from all over India ensure the execution of its tradition in the service of the *sarvagyapeeth*. If any scholar considers himself to be an administrator of the omniscient *peeth*, then he has to arrive at *sarvagyapeeth* to make an announcement. At the four entrances of the *sarvagyapeeth*, the best scholars have to be defeated in debate and only then is the verdict for omniscience declared.

In the last extended time, exceptional abbots and *mahamahopadhyas* (honorific title given to exceptional scholars) had come here with a desire to be seated on the *sarvagya* seat but could not become victorious. The leading seniormost Brahmins in their known memory have not seen anyone on the *sarvagya* (all knowing) seat and even their ancestors had seen the omniscient *peeth* vacant during their times.

Sarvagyapeeth has been waiting since ages for someone meritorious, virtuous and knower of *Vedas* to arrive and sit on this *peeth* and give it a meaning. Acharya Shankar and his team reach Srinagar after crossing the inaccessible mountains, but the warm welcome by the residents of Srinagar eases their fatigue and hard toil of the journey.

Acharya chooses to stay on the banks of River Krishnaganga in the shade of tall and majestic *chinar* and *deodar* trees. The *pandits* of Kashmir are proud of their superiority, so how can they accept someone else as their chief? They do not even want to listen to the teachings of Acharya Shankar!

On the request of the king, they have followed the tradition of welcoming the guests but they are not ready to give any importance to anyone else. And why should they give? They have learned and practiced for more than the age of Acharya. They are not only well versed in *Agama, Nigam, Purana, Shruti, sangeet* but also in *vaidaki*, meteorology, botany, etc. So, how can the peaks of Kashmir bow their proud heads in front of Shankar?

Acharya discusses all these issues with his disciples and after careful discussion concludes that the only one way to face the resistance and arrogance of Kashmiri *pandits* is to throne their *guru* on the omniscient *peeth*. Whoever opposes or hinders has to be defeated in debate. At the request of the disciples, Acharya consents and a senior disciple is deputed to the *sarvagyapeeth* to announce the resolution of Acharya. The announcement by the messenger of Acharya on the *sarvagyapeeth* causes an uproar. The best teachers assigned to protect the dignity and tradition of the *peeth* call an emergency meeting to discuss the proposal made by Acharya. It is decided to summon Acharya next morning. No one is able to sleep that night in the *sarvagyapeeth*. All the learned scholars are engaged in planning the next day's strategy. On the other hand, Acharya and his disciples, content at the acceptance of their proposal, have gone into deep sleep on the banks of the river.

Next day, Acharya leaves to go to *sarvagyapeeth*. Accompanying him is his group of disciples. The citizens of

Srinagar are amazed to see the congregation of monks, who look energetic, vibrant young disciples dressed in saffron robes and marching along the path in a disciplined manner. They are lined up and their physique shows that they are not mere spiritualists but possess muscular strength. The townpeople have counted that there are three thousand young ascetics and senior citizens tell the youth and teenagers that they had seen such an assembly only at the Kumbh fair.

At this, a young man says, "No, there are many thousands of them. I myself have seen their resting place on the bank of Krishnaganga river; it seems as if a city of huts and tents has set up camp there."

Another eyewitness remarks, "The work of building huts and tents was going on there the last fortnight."

Today the whole city is marching towards *sarvagyapeeth*. Even before the arrival of Acharya, learned *pandits* have gathered around the *peeth*. As soon as Acharya reaches, way is made for him. When he reaches the eastern gate of the *peeth*, the *pandits* gathered there challenge him, preventing him from entering, "O ascetic, this is *sarvagyapeeth*. The sun of many scholars has set here. Are you sure of your omniscience?"

Raising his head, Acharya looks straight at the *pandits* who are blocking the door and says with confidence, "Gentlemen, I, Shankar, the supreme disciple of Gaur Padacharya, raise my arm and claim that by *guru's* grace, I am the knower of all the scriptures and no branch of learning is unknown to me. Those who have doubts are invited to test me."

One by one the scholars who follow the sects of Kanada, Gautam, Kapil, Jaimini, etc. come forward to debate but bow their heads in dejection on getting defeated in front of the wisdom of Acharya. The losers include Jains, Buddhists, Charvakas and Nihilists. The people watch Acharya render scholars speechless with astonishment and joy in this series of debates. All the *pandits* are unanimously satisfied at the arguments put forth by Acharya.

They request him to sit on the omniscient seat.

The euphoria reaches its peak as soon as he mounts the Sharda Peeth. A child monk, who had begun his journey from Kaladi in South India now occupies the Sharda Peeth in North India with the dignity of his knowledge and the brilliance of youth.

He is lustily cheered by the local citizens as well as the distinguished scholars of Sharda Peeth as they had been waiting for generations to find a suitable incarnation to fill this seat. Acharya himself is very happy. This marks an unforgettable success of his victorious march. Now south and north of India are tied in the thread of monism.

Mounting the *sarvagyapeeth* leads to a tremendous psychological impact on Kashmiri *pandits*. They now stand in line to pay their homage to Acharya, whereas Acharya is honoured to have climbed a high hill in Srinagar with his disciples. When he returns from there, signs of the tedious task of mountaineering are visible on his face. He is happy to have met the proud, intelligent, cultured *pandits* of Kashmir with utmost respect and draws the plan for the future.

He says, "Today I have selected the site on this high hill of Srinagar. If you all agree, it is my resolve to establish a temple of Lord Shiva over here."

All the *pandits* voice their agreement. After staying for a month, Acharya arranges for teaching of monism in the *sarvagyapeeth* as well as starting the construction of the Shiva temple on the hill at an auspicious time. The Srinagar plaintiffs offer ready cooperation in the establishment of the temple and a new Shiva temple begins to take shape on the highest peak of the hill.

The local people have great faith in an ancient Devi temple near Srinagar. Acharya also visits the shrine with his disciples to pay homage to the goddess. The chief priest takes him affectionately to the sanctorum. Here Acharya's heart becomes so overwhelmed on seeing the lively idol of the goddess that poetry overflows from his melodious throat. Not only the chief priest, even the other devotees get mesmerised on hearing such a captivating verse. His disciples savour this instant poetic juice emerging like nectar from the lips of their unique *guru*.

Their *guru's* throat echoes, "O goddess, when Shiva is empowered with Shakti, then only he is capable of creation, construction and destruction; otherwise even the Supreme God cannot pulsate:

Shiv: shaktaya yukto yadi bhavati shakt; prabhvitum
n davebam devo n khulkushala: spanditumari!!"

The disciples are always ready to drink the pleasure of the poetic talent of their beloved *guru*, but owing to the busy schedule of their master, they are left thirsty. But whenever the stream of poetry flows from his heart and spills from the lips, it becomes a joyous occasion for them. The melodious voice and the perfect utterances of poetry of the highest order find comfort even in the detached and dry minds of sages and ascetics.

Today the same coincidence occurs at this temple of the goddess. The best verses spring from his throat, one after another and the listeners rejoice in this blissful river of poetic *rasa*.

After the completion of more than a hundred verses, Acharya rests his voice and the people present there return to the reality of their mundane life. Padmapada requests in a humble manner, "Gurudev, in this poetic flow lies a unique description of the beauty and power of the goddess. By what name will we refer to this holy source?"

Deep in ecstasy, Acharya replies, "Today this source has appeared by itself in the temple of Ashadevi Girija Bhavani. You and the rest of the world will know it as *Saundarya Lahiri*."

This *Saundarya Lahiri* by Acharya Shankar continues to satisfy the devotees for a few days in the form of a chorus in the temple. The people of Kashmir now begin to show more reverence to the Acharya. The purpose of coming to Kashmir gets fulfilled. Acharya now returns to the Gangetic plains by marching forward to Nemisharanya via Takshashila, Jwalamukhi and Haridwar. The spots where they stop and rest in the due course of their journey become special after their departure. The same has happened in Srinagar. At the foot of the hill, where he rested and consecrated the *shivalinga* on the summit is named Shankaracharya Hill by the local dwellers. His fame keeps on to multiply day and night in the hearts of the public.

□

60

Once at Nemisharanya

Acharya and his disciples are both astonished and grieved to reach Nemisharanya, the major centre of Vedic culture during ancient times as it has undergone a complete transformation over the course of time. Present there are neither *ashrams* of sages, nor the fragrant smoke from *yajna* pavilions. No one exactly remembers when the *Vedas* were recited for the last time. With his own eyes, Acharya notices the supremacy of Buddhist *tantrics*. He resolves there and then to culturally revive this pilgrimage centre. The local Buddhists also comprehend his point that change in faith does not change the culture. He wins over the minds of the local Buddhists through logic arguments and their hearts with his melodious voice.

Through constant efforts he is successful in making them understand that the path of knowledge shown by Mahatama Buddha is nothing but monism. Due to the bright conduct and adorable speech of his disciples, Nemisharanya now returns to its Vedic roots.

Acharya leaves for Ayodhya after he sees the smoke billowing out from the *yajna* centres and the *ashrams* of Nemisharanya. The hearts of the saints are ecstatic on their way to Ayodhya, which is situated on the banks of the beautiful River Saryu. Before setting their feet on the birthplace of Maryada Purushottam Lord Rama, all salute him with reverence. There is no one in the group whose heart does not fill with devotion at this place.

The enthusiasm of the pilgrims at Ayodhya *darshan* turns

into despair as soon as they enter the city. No one is present to welcome them and neither does anyone awaits them, nor is anyone desirous of meeting them. It is nice on the part of Acharya to have planned the outline of the journey and the spots to camp in advance that this victory march is able to stay in Ayodhya. Some of the monks who have reached in advance make arrangements for shade, rest, drinking water, food, building, etc. as a result of which the pilgrims do not face any inconvenience through negligence. Acharya's umbrella of care has taught each of them how to behave in front of public. Both praise and condemnation do not affect them.

Their focus remains either on the goal or on their *guru* Acharya whom they love more than life. The disciples, including Acharya, are shocked to witness that worship of the deities in the temple has become a taboo because of the strong influence of Buddhism. No one exactly remembers when the prayer bells rang last time in the temple of Lord Ram. The entire Ayodhya has become *'Buddham sharanam gacchami'* in such a manner that even if Lord Ram were to himself arrive, he would begin to doubt if he has come to the right place!

The advance squad of Acharya has arranged lodging in the dense mango grove on the banks of River Saryu. The team has stayed here. They have already toured the entire city. There are many spots related to the life events of Lord Ram and his great family, but now lie badly neglected, unhygienic and deserted because Ayodhya has become Buddhist in mind, word and deed.

Acharya and his disciples begin to contemplate on how to make this Buddhist Ayodhya return to the Ayodhya of Lord Ram. Acharya is seated on a platform while his dear disciples surround him. Padmapada, Sureshacharya, Hastamalak, Totak are contemplating on the challenge they confront in Ayodhya. After listening to everyone's opinions and suggestions, Acharya puts forth his decision in a solemn voice, "Lord Buddha raised voice against such defects in Sanatan Dharma, which have plagued the entire society, so his message of peace was magical for the conflict-stricken people. Buddhism began to rule the mind because practically everyone needed this. Mahatma Buddha had ruled not only over the public mind, but also over the kings and the wealthy class with his amiable conduct, sharp arguments and skilled public dealing. This is the real reason for the rapid advance of Buddhism. It is not wise to suppress Buddhists with muscle power; after all, they are like a stream emanating from the huge river of Sanatan Dharma.

"The hatred they have for Sanatan Dharma cannot be conquered by hatred. Lord Buddha himself has said that we can conquer hatred with love. If we include Lord Buddha among our incarnations and worship him, then Buddhists can be brought back to the mainstream." Saying this, Acharya turns silent for a moment and there reigns an atmosphere of complete peace. His learned and humble disciples look at his face and listen attentively to his sermon.

Acharya continues, "I consider Lord Gautam Buddha as the ninth incarnation of Lord Vishnu. If we inculcate this fact in the mind of general public, especially in that of the Buddhists who are fierce about their identity, then the animosity of the Buddhists will diminsh."

Each disciple agrees by nodding his head unanimously and the history of Ayodhya once again returns to its Sanatan roots. During the long stay of Acharya and his disciples, the people of Ayodhya get bound in monism and respect for Gautam Buddha increases among the Sanatan followers. The Sri Ram temple of Ayodhya again reverberates with life. One can hear the chants of both *'Buddham sharanam gacchami'*, and *'Ram Ram, Sita Ram'* in Ayodhya.

After the unique success of Ayodhya, Acharya's victory march proceeds ahead, blowing the *mantra* of monism in the ears of the public. The pilgrims arrive in Gaya after sharing the message of coordination, cooperation and love in Mithila, Magadha, Nalanda,

Rajgriha. At one time, Mithila was ruled majestically by the royal sage-like Videh Raja Janak who had fallen under the influence of Buddha's magical message; similar was the case in Magadha, Nalanda and Rajgriha which had become admirers of Tathagata. Here the roots of Buddhism were very strong because these areas had seen Buddha with their own eyes and heard him with their ears. In every age, the subjects of the warring kings had breathed a sigh of relief after receiving Buddha's message of peace. Today, when Acharya Shankar has set foot on the same soil, the age-old memories have come alive. Suddenly everywhere in Magadha, Nalanda, Rajgriha, the memory of Lord Buddha gets revived on seeing Acharya. Ahh! What a splendid personality, beautiful body, glowing face with aura, dazzling eyes, fragrant and loving voice that cools the ears. One who sees, becomes enchanted and one who hears, feels close to him.

Such an effective personality belonged only to Gautam Buddha, whose speech and personality had completely conquered the complex and fragmented society of India. Now the same responsibility has fallen on the young shoulders of Acharya Shankar. Gautam Buddha had uprooted the distortions that had entered the Vedic religion, but when the enthusiasm and arrogance of his disciples chose to eradicate the eternal Sanatan religion, the same divine authority has arrived now in the form of Acharya Shankar to establish the Sanatan truth. In this act of giving a new lease of life to the everlasting culture through his victory march, the next goal is the ancient pilgrimage centre of Gaya.

Since ages, the followers of Vedic culture from every corner of India had been visiting Gaya to seek salvation for their ancestors. Since ancient times, the *gadadshara* form of Lord Vishnu has been worshipped in Gaya. It is the sacred duty of every son to do *pindadan* (offering to the dead elders) with devotion in Gaya because without doing so, the ancestors cannot achieve *moksha* (salvation). That is why Gaya has become a pilgrimage centre for Vedic culture and a fort for spreading the tradition of charity.

Mahashraman Gautam Buddha had attained enlightenment near Gaya under the Bodhi tree. Due to his splendour, the place had become famous as Bodh Gaya, overcoming the importance and dignity of ancient Gaya. Emperor Ashoka had enshrined a philosophical idol of Mahatma Buddha in a huge and grand temple at Bodh Gaya. Since then, Bodh Gaya has become an essential and holiest pilgrimage for Buddhists from all over the world. In practice, Bodh Gaya is a symbol of the authority and power of Buddhism. It is here that when Acharya Shankar reaches with the victory flag of monism, an unknown fear grips the minds of Buddhists. After all, his fame lies in his being anti-Buddhist in nature and a supporter of the *Vedas*.

Some Buddhists get ready to counter Acharya Shankar on speaking against Lord Gautam Buddha or against the path propounded by him. Some more zealous ones even collect stones, sticks, balls that if the Acharya's logic were to fall short, then violence would be their logic.

On reaching Bodh Gaya, Acharya goes straight to the idol of Lord Gautam Buddha to pay his respects with reverence in the Buddhist temple. The chief priest is astonished to see the Acharya, who has become popular for being anti-Buddha, worship Lord Buddha and get immersed in devotion!

After offering his prayers, Acharya steps out. The Buddhists present in the temple courtyard greet him with courtesy and plead with him to address the public. As desired, Acharya begins to speak in his harmonious voice, rendering all the noise and unrest to subside. He says, "I bow to the Supreme Lord residing in your souls, in the holy temple of Lord Buddha, the ninth incarnation of Lord Vishnu. Not only to our great land, but Lord Buddha has shown the path of liberation to entire humanity against the web of violence, malice, mutual conflict, enmity, differences among the high and low. His teachings uphold the same values of equality in which our great sages and ascetics have breathed life through tireless penance."

Every statement of his is applauded. He continues, "The enmity between Vedic religion and Buddhism is baseless; Lord Buddha himself was a follower of Sanatan religion. He opposed the distortions that had arisen in Vedic religion and it is a sin to consider him anti-*Veda*..." He adds, "Sanatan Dharma considers salvation as the aim of life while Buddha considered *nirvana* as the ultimate truth. Please tell me that apart from terminology, what is the difference between these two terms?"

With his eloquence he is successful in eliminating the doubts in the Buddhist minds. Those who have collected stones and sticks to kill him are humbled and bow down to take the soil of his feet. However, his declaration of Gautam Buddha as the ninth incarnation of Vishnu is strongly opposed by some hypocritical sects who call him a 'disguised Buddhist', but the majority accept him as genuine. The Sanatanis who had begun to worship Buddha and the Buddhists too now start to reconnect with the Sanatan identity. This successful attempt at national integration is repeated all over the country. The new message of unity that emerges from Bodh Gaya now reverberates across the country. The lifeless Sanatan centres of Gaya come to life again in the presence of Acharya.

Taking a heartfelt farewell from the Sanatan culture and Buddhists of Gaya, this eternal pilgrim now proceeds towards Bengal.

□

61

Cheers in Bengal

Acharya Shankar, who had so far easily covered most of India on foot like the Vamana *avatar*, now reaches Bengal with his disciples. The news of his arrival sends a strong wave of enthusiasm among the people living from River Ganga to River Padma. Abundant images of Acharya – as a revolutionary, social reformer, forerunner of new awakening, facilitator of national integration, rebel monk, wonderful preacher of Vedanta, mesmerising *rasa-siddha* poet, modern sage, public speaker, scholar of *Vedas* – can be seen all over! How long Bengal had been waiting for this relentless pilgrim to arrive!

The last time he had visited Puri, a ray of hope had illuminated in the minds of the people of Bengal and Kamrup that this epoch-making religious *guru* would show the way to eradicate evil practices like incest, magic, violent *tantras* that had been flourishing in eastern India, but their hopes were dashed when he failed to visit them.

After a long wait, the auspicious message of his arrival was spreading waves in Bengal, the holy land of knowledge and devotion.

The public welcomed the team of devotees who reached ahead of Acharya with great enthusiasm. A huge mass of people gathered to listen to them. Then Acharya arrives and he satisfies the religious curiosity of the public in simple yet effective words. He explains the rationale behind the worship of five gods and five great sacrifices. He enchants the audience with interesting stories from the *Puranas*.

When the pure Sanskrit hymns of the South Indian *sadhus* are recited by the disciples, after the musical performance of devotional singers of Bengal, everyone gets drenched in the rain of happiness. The people go crazy with joy on hearing the glories of various incarnations of God from the throats of the chorus singers of Maharashtra, of Vrindavan for singing praise of Krishna and for the folk-singers of Mithilanchal.

At every halt of Acharya, people flow in like a flood and in every spiritual discourse, people are satisfied to hear about the principle of monism, the attack on hypocrisy, the differences between the high and low and the message of social harmony. One group of his disciples creates mass awakening by training the local priests and enthusiastic youth, while the second group gives useful suggestions to the royalty regarding the progress of their state. A third group talks about the financial outcome of social harmony with businessmen and wealthy people. In this group of disciples are present experts in Ayurveda who treat the people and suggest ways to stay healthy.

The natural outcome of these related efforts is visible in the form of social harmony, salvation of temples and encouragement of local talent. Leaving an indelible imprint on the minds of the people and awakening them, the group proceeds towards the next destination. Competent persons in the crew are given the responsibility of carrying out coordination and continuous activism. Some people from the local community are selected and included in the group.

After awakening Bengal and confirming the Vedic way, the team is now moving towards a more difficult goal. Karmrup is an unpierced fort of *tantrics*. The triangle formed on the land running from River Karleya to River Brahmaputra is known as Kamrup. Kamakhyapeeth is its most important and most powerful monastery. In this unbroken kingdom of the worshippers of

Shakti, a seeker of other *mantra* cannot dare to enter.

Abhinavagupta is the head of these fiery and brilliant *tantrics*. He is a Brahmin by birth and a *guru* in *tantra* practice. He worships goddess, hates weakness and mild expressions. He considers non-violence of Buddhists to be cowardice and hypocrisy. Acharya Shankar's gentleness incites him. He detests peace and harmony because it is the cause of defeat and downfall of the nation. He does not want to nurture patience to win the hearts of the enemies. Destruction of the enemy holds chivalric value for him. He is the worshipper of the supreme power, the world's mother goddess who is the destroyer of evil; other gods and goddesses are of negligible importance to him. He is very angry with the worshlip of five deities as propagated by Acharya. He had sent a challenge to Acharya for debate during his stay in Srinagar.

In his monastery, animals are constantly sacrificed in front of the idol of the goddess and every day a river of blood flows out. The people even discuss in subdued voices the worth of human sacrifice. Now, with the arrival of Acharya, Abhinavagupta wants to show that the morale of Shaktas has reached by defeating the former in debate. His followers are also fierce and aggressive like him. The anger of the *tantrics* is visible in the form of dry behaviour even while welcoming Acharya at the Kamakhya temple.

When Acharya reaches the pavilion of the main temple to see the goddess, he is stunned to see the stream of blood, hear the screams of sacrificial animals and the offerings of meat. The flies buzzing on the blood make the scene all the more gory and unbearable. The mute animals tied in ropes and chains are brought in before the goddess. With the worship, the animals are killed in one blow with a huge dagger that chops the head to suffer on the ground on getting separated from the body. Even the loud cheers of the devotees are unable to hide the heart-rending groans of the speechless creature. This gruesome scene of bloodshed and animal killing renders Acharya and his disciples unhappy while the *tantrics* display a triumphant smile on their faces.

Within a few moments, Acharya controls his emotions and bows down to the goddess and praises her by singing hymns in her praise. It is not an easy task in this torturous place. In the name of religion, the temple has been made into a place of slaughter of speechless creatures. Many pilgrims faint on seeing this horrific sight. The arrogance of the *tantrics* increases on seeing these cowards faint.

After worshipping for a few moments, Acharya sits down on the seat for debate. While starting the debate, Abhinavagupta describes mercy, forgiveness, tolerance as the cause of national weakness in the country. He justifies the worship of Shakti and describes monism as useless and nonsense. In the same breath, he calls the worship of the primitive Goddess Shakti as religious. He tries to prove that everything else is hypocrisy.

Describing the attainment of salvation through the path of austerity and displaying his knowledge, Acharya asks, "The one who is the merciful mother of all the creatures of the world and is the mother of the world, how can she drink the blood of her own children?"

Ultimately Abhinavagupta accepts defeat and Acharya initiates him as a disciple. The news of the defeat of Abhinavagupta and his initiation as a disciple spreads everywhere with the speed of light, including in Bengal and Tripura. The *tantrics* leave behind their practice of animal slaughter and the victory of reason over the sword spreads the popularity of Acharya from village to village.

There is a spirit of great enthusiasm among the new disciples who are anxious to leave the old disciples behind. Same is the case with Navagupta who remains in the shadow of his *guru* from morning till night. All the old disciples are apprehensive of this immense love and service by him but then the question is how to alert their *guru*?

Guru Acharya, the idol of love, is simplehearted and is not

at all worried about the danger lurking behind this service. The disciples think that Abhinavagupta, afer his defeat in logic, will harm their *guru* any day. Once again this responsibility falls on Padmapada's head to save the life of Acharya through preventive meassures.

Padmapada warns his *guru* when they are together that he should be cautious of his new devotee. Guru replies, "I understand your affection, but our victory is governed by faith, not by doubt. This body is temporary and mortal. Why worry so much about it? If Abhinavagupta wants to betray me even after being with me, it means that my penance has been lacking in some way and the new disciple is not in the wrong."

Feeling defeated, Padmapada returns, fixed the duties of the disciples to remain alert and keep an eye on Abhinavagupta's activities.

On the request of Abhinavagupta, Acharya sets out on a journey to the Shakti *peeths* of South Bengal. Abhinavagupta has good knowledge of this area and takes Acharya to a place called Chattal. It is a popular belief that the left arm of Goddess Parvati fell here. Bhairav Chandrashekhar's temple has been built here. Some distance away from here, the left palm of Goddess Parvati had fallen and here stands the temple of Goddess Yashoshwari.

Acharya does not like the climate here and feels unwell. He has come far from Kerala, crossing Himachal to Tibet. He has also travelled in fierce heat and desert of Gurjar country and Rajputana. While ascending to the top of Sahyadri and descending down towards Gandhara and Takshashila, he has measured the five rivers. Nowhere ever had he felt weak but in Bengal and in Kamarup he feels enervated. Above all, here the food is also strange. Anyway, he takes a balanced diet but the amount has fallen to nominal and whatever he takes seems foreign to him. Even the water seems distasteful – strange, muddy water of the springs, that neither satisfies nor is cool.

Bearing this restlessness and inconvenience, when he reaches the temple of Tara Devi on the banks of River Sunanda, he feels completely unwell. He finds it difficult to walk even a single step. His disciples are unable to see this condition of their revered *guru* and so desperately send news of his health to the ruler of Bengal, who has unwavering faith in Acharya. They are certain that the king would arrange the best for Acharya in the temple premises.

The next evening, Acharya continues to writhe in severe pain. The doctor in service of the royal family is sent for by the king. The royal physician examines Acharya's health in solitude and advises the patient to take complete rest. He warns, "You are debilitated by constant pain and bleeding, but there is no need to worry. You will be in perfect health with my medicine."

For a few days, Acharya takes care of his health and without recuperating fully goes towards the Kali *peeth*, where the rest of his disciples are waiting for him. The disciples crowd around him as soon as he arrives while the local citizens are happy to see Acharya. The disciples however are pained to see the weak body of their *guru*.

The crowds of devotees start gathering for Acharya at Kali *peetha*. Even before the discourse begins, there is no place for .Acharya to sit. Space is cleared for him and he teaches them the *mantra* of monism Vedanta. Tolerance has begun to take the place of social discrimination and animosity. Innumerable people meet him regularly after the discourse to seek his blessings and tell him about their happiness and worries. Everyone wants to get initiated by him and he does not let anyone down.

There is a large number of people wanting to seek initiation. People in queue come with coconut and sweets in their hands. They have reverence in their heart and are prepared to surrender faith at the feet of *guruji*. *Guruji* initiates them with love. Then a senior disciple comes and requests, "Gurudev, a group of Vedic scholars from Nepal, the holy land of Lord Pashupatinath, has come to visit you, but they want to see you alone."

Acharya replies affectionately, "Make suitable arrangements

for the guests and accord them due hospitality. After *gurudiksha*, I shall meet them in my hut. Today I will take dinner only after holding a discussion with them."

The disciples return after saying, "As you command, Gurudev." Acharya gets engrossed in initiating the devotees, advising them to resolve to do good deeds and try to renounce at least one vice from their life.

As soon as the initiation work completes, Acharya goes to the room, where the scholars from Nepal are waiting for him. All of them touch his feet one by one and receive his blessings. When the Acharya takes a piece of confectionary kept near him as *prasad*, they become glad. On receiving the signal from Acharya to speak, the chief of the delegation begins, "O great Acharya, you have revived the Vedic culture through toil and patience. From the plateau of Tibet to the southern peninsula, Gandhara, Kaikeya, Valmiki, Gurjar, Saurashtra, Maharashtra, you have illuminated the public mind by dispelling the darkness of innumerable temples in all the four directions. The most revered Acharya Shankar from the wonderful sage tradition of India, we have come here with a prayer to you. Please make the next halt of your victorious journey in Kathmandu."

After this, the scholars narrate in detail the plight of the temple of Lord Pashupatinath and the weakness that lies in the learning of the *Vedas* in Nepal and its surrounding region. Acharya assures them that his next stop would only be Kathmandu. After taking his meal with the guests, Acharya retires for the day and the delegates return to Kathmandu with pleasure.

Acharya, along with some senior disciples, finalises the outline of his tour of Nepal after the workshop in the evening.

The advance group is instructed early in the day to leave the next day and manage the route. The devotees of Kali *peeth* become sad as soon as they receive the news of Acharya leaving for Nepal after three days. They become sad to learn that the time for completion of the celebration ceremony of devotion, gaiety and knowledge draws near for Acharya's departure.

Acharya reaches Nepal via Magadha along with his disciples after consoling everyone. The difficulties on the way weigh heavy on his health, but he is not willing to ignore the call of his duty. He considers the body a means of *dharma*, an instrument for the worship of God. He has no attachment to his body; even though he is in the body, he is untouched by it.

To welcome him in Kathmandu, people of all religions and all faiths have gathered. All feel that they had never seen such a large crowd in their life. The sun of Acharya's fame shines here too with full majesty. Everybody wants to derive energy from him. Seeing such a devotional spirit of the crowd, Acharya forgets all about his ailment and his face begins to glow with unique brilliance.

To the Buddhists, it seems as if Gautama Buddha has come again to earth; to the Shaivas, he appears as Lord Shiva and to the Vaishnavas as Vishnu, the maintainer of the world. His mere presence gives life to the withering creepers of the Vedic path and turn green. The bells in the temples start ringing, lamps and prayers brighten the day. The religious discord in Nepal has been quelled. In his discourses, Buddhists have a direct experience of Buddha, Shaivas of Shiva element and Shaktas of Shakti.

The temple of Lord Pashupatinath is getting decorated. Acharya's *mantra* of harmony in all religions, respect for all has been assimilated by everyone. With Nepal becoming religious, Acharya and his disciples are now preparing to go on to Kailash Mansarovar.

From Kathmandu to Tanakpur, Pithoragarh, Aaskor, Dharchool, Garkhyang, Kalapani, etc., the local people welcome the pilgrims with fanfare. The programme of daily religious preaching, private meetings also become very popular. One of the characteristics of Acharya is that his basic routine is very systematic. Wherever he stays, his regular routine like bathing, meditation, worship, self-study, sermons and training of disciples remains same. There is not even the slightest difference in his programme despite the changing circumstances. He performs with determination the proposed task at the appointed time and day.There is no reason to procastinate.

After many days of continuous journey, they now reach a deserted plateau. When crossing it diligently, they are enthralled at the beauty of a very captivating lake. This huge lake is very beautiful. Acharya tells his disciples, "This beautiful lake is Rakshastaal. It is said that the demon-king Ravana meditated here."

The journey starts again from the Rakshastaal and the next stop is at Mansarovar, whose limitless natural beauty is seen to be believed. It is here that Sati's right palm fell; hence this place is also treated as a Shakti *peeth*. Acharya informs his disciples that poet Valmiki, while describing Mansarovar in the epic *Ramayana*, says, "O Rama, the lake created from the mind of Brahma on Mount Kailash is Mansarovar." The glory of this place is described in various *Puranas* and scriptures.

A camp is set up for resting on the banks of Mansarovar. After resting here for a night, the very next day the team moves towards Mount Kailash.The pilgrims are taken in by the enchanting beauty of Mount Kailash after a long journey. Due to its magnificence, the Kailash mountain is visible from a distance, looking like a *shivalinga* made from snow. The rays of the sun decorate it in rainbow colours, making the pilgrims forget their fatigue on looking at Mount Kailash with awe. Since the oxygen level is low on the mountains, ordinary householders are liable to suffer from breathlessness but the *yogis* do not face much difficulty because they are able to enjoy the benefits of *yoga* and *pranayama*. Acharya's disciples, while moving over the inaccessible snowy mountains, realise the benefits of their discipline gained by performing *pranayama* and *yogasanas* every day.

Prior to beginniing the circumambulation of Kailash, Acharya reveals to his disciples, "This Kailash mountain is a symbol of the universe. This part of land surrounded by mountains resembles a *yoni*. In the centre, the Kailash mountain stands like a phallus, symbolising that creation started through the union of Nature with man. The satisfaction at the visit to Kailash mountain prepares the group for the return journey as it is anxious to return to the plains after crossing the rural areas of Tibet. Acharya has seen his *guru* in his dream and thus seems very pleased and satisfied. The *guru* is seen telling Acharya after making him sit lovingly beside him, "Shankar, you have performed your duty well but now you have to give a permanent institutional form to your life's labour as you are nearing completion of your life. This is your thirty-second year by way of age, so now you should go to Badrinath and preach the message of monism in the inaccessible areas around Badrinath as a final offering towards your goal."

The dream breaks as soon as Acharya awakens. The happy moments in his *guru's* company pass as soon as his eyes open and the harsh realities of life await him at Badrinath.

In the morning, when he narrates the episode of his dream to the disciples, the eyes of the celibates, who have renounced the shackles of the world, fill with tears and they find themselves not as free as they were supposed to be. They too realise that their *guru* would not always be with them as he is nearing completion of his life, though no one is willing to accept this truth.

The pilgrims move towards Badrinath. On reaching the dilapidated condition of the temple, Acharya and his disciples are unable to remain silent spectators. They decide to get down to work. Crowds of devotees gather around them as the disciples clear the debris and repair the temple. It is only after the immersion of the broken idols and the consecration of the new idol that they proceed towards the next halt. They take rest in Srinagar, after which they reach Devprayag. They cover Rudraprayag, Karnprayag, Nandprayag where this great effort of Acharya takes the form of a mass movement. Acharya says, "Temples are not mere places of worship; they are the centres of consciousness of our culture where education, rituals, health, astrology, time-calculation, collectivism and socialisation flourish.

"Our dance, music, painting, singing, sculpture, jewellery, culinary art have all developed as part of the temple activities. They are living centres of employment, business, gardening, handicraft, social science as well as exchange of information. They are also sites which act as centres for resolving disputes. Temples cannot be allowed to be destroyed."

Acharya's *mantra* of renaissance reverberates in the mountains. The temples are renovated and rebuilt by the common masses who start cleaning, repairing, painting and consecrating the temples through mutual cooperation, donations and free labour. Worship, *yajna* and mass banquets are organised in the temples. Now there is no shortage of ingredients for burning in the *yajnas* and even the new generation has started going to temples for education.

Kumaon and Garhwal are revered as God's lands in the Himalayas. With the arrival of Acharya in the land of gods, even the fortune of the deities has awakened.

From Nandprayag, this team of religious warriors moves towards Joshimath, where the disciples rest at a pleasant spot. Acharya rests in a natural cave adjacent to the camp. His mind is pleased to see the beautiful Kalpa tree outside the cave and he decides to meditate under the same tree from the next day.

The local king and subjects have great reverence for Acharya and thus have made grand arrangements for his welcome. The king himself is present for his arrival. Acharya blesses him and calls for a detailed discussion the next day as he is tired that day.

When the king arrives the next day, Acharya indicates his desire to make Joshimath a *jyotirpeeth*. The king accepts his offer with his mind and heart.

□

62

Four Monastries, Four Sentinels

Today's main question during the discussions with his intimate disciples is who should be appointed as the first presiding officer of Dwarkapeeth. There are equally exceptional, devoted and learned meditators among the disciples blessed with good conduct, purity, intelligence, reasoning power and all other qualities. Dwarkapeeth is to become the first *peeth*. The new energy to Sanatan Dharma has to be transmitted from here, therefore the selection is not easy. A vast area is about to come under the Dwarkapeeth. Indus, Sauvir (Kutch), Saurashtra, Kathiawad, Maharashtra and central India will now fall under the jurisdiction of the Sharda Math located in the west. The residents of all these areas are intelligent, relatively rich, deeply cultured and with a strong insistence on their opinion. Therefore, Shankaracharya's thinking is directed towards anointing and appointing a very intelligent person who is not only brilliant but has leadership qualities to guide the local residents. He should also be able to establish the supremacy of Dwarkapeeth through his sharp wit and rationality. From this point of view, Sureshvara seems most suitable among all his disciples. So he decides to entrust this responsibility to Sureshvara.

□

63

Sharda Math / Dwarkapeeth

Adi Shankar, who now shines like the sun amidst his disciples, speaks to them, "The first study centre established by me will be in the west direction. It will be called Sharda Math. The name of this region is Dwarka and the deity at this place is Siddeshwar and the goddess is Bhadrakali. Its *acharya* has to be nominated. In view of the geographical and mental challenges here, I nominate Vishwaroop as the first *acharya* of this Math.'

The disciples welcome the *guru's* command with jubilation.

□

64

Govardhan Math at Puri

Adi Shankar says, "The spot where Lord Jagannath is seated is known as Purushottam. Here, as the observer of Sanatan Dharma, I aim to establish Govardhan Math. The area of this monastery will cover Bengal, Kalinga, Magadha, Utkal and the forest provinces. In this entire region, there is a predominance of fish eating and drink consuming. Here, when the fanatics start getting defeated in debates, they stoop down to adopting illogical statements. Padmapada will be able to control them with his wisdom and courage. That's why I appoint him as the caretaker of Govardhan Peeth."

□

65

Jyotirmath / Badrikashram

The Dwarka Math is established in the west and Govardhan Math in the east. Now is the turn of the north about which Adi Shankar tells his disciples, "I want to establish Jyotirmath in Badrikashram for the guidance and control of the area in the north. All the states of North India will be in the domain of Jyotirmath and Lord Badrinarayan will be its deity. This region belongs to *yogis* and *rishis* since ancient times. That is why I have chosen to appoint Yogiraj Totak among my disciples as the abbot of Jyotirmath."

□

66
Shringeri Math

After establishing monasteries on the east, west and north of India, it is the turn of South India. Adi Shankar decides to establish a monastery at Shringeri in south. He tells his disciples, "The various regions of Andhra, Dravida, Karnataka, Kerala, etc. which are located in South India will fall under the aegis of Shringeri Math. This area of serene beauty will attract serious devotees. Therefore, the supremely simple saint Hastamalak will serve as *acharya* here."

With the establishment of the four monasteries, a new wave of enthusiasm spreads in the entire nation. Sanatan Dharma begins to embrace the blush of new youth. With the establishment of four monasteries in all four directions, Vedanta comes to be idolised everywhere, but with the addition of over-zealous followers to the new system, there arise new problems.

Thus, there is a need to enforce some discipline and rules for the smooth functioning of this newly established system. In this way no monastery and no *acharya* would have to waste his energy in dominating over others. At the same time, no monastery would become inactive or languish. So Adi Shankar chalks out detailed rules for the establishment of monasteries and in which the qualifications of the leader, the nature of work as well as a constitution in daily practice are listed. He divides the four *Vedas* among the four *maths,* giving different names to the sages and the monks of the four monasteries. The responsibility of teaching and propagating *Samaveda* is placed on Sharda Math, while

Govardhan monastery is given the responsibility of spreading *Rigveda.* The Jyotirmath is made responsible for preaching the *Atharveda* and Shringeri monastery is assigned the responsibility of the *Yajurveda*. All the monasteries are provided separate *tirthas* and *mahavakyas* The holy place for Sharda Math is designated as Gomti and *Tattvamasi* becomes the slogan. Pilgrim Mahodadhi and the slogan *Pragyanam Brahma* is given to Govardhan Math, holy place Alaknanda and slogan *Ayamatma* is given to Jyotirmath and pilgrimage Tungabhadra is given to Shringeri Math with the slogan *Aham Brahmasmi.*

Two days later, this delegation of Acharya and his disciples reaches Adi-Badri where a temple and black stone idol of Badrinarayan has been established. The remaining work is completed by the king's employees. The team proceeds towards Heelang to reach the deserted and isolated temple of Buddha Badri or Old Badri. Acharya cleans up the place and spends a day here in worship. From Helaang they reach Urgaam, where Acharya establishes the idol of Lord Kedarnath and inaugurates the construction of the temple. From Pandukeshwar to Hanuman Chatti, he proceeds towards Badri Vishal. From Akshaytritiya to Badrinath, he comes to the temple and stays here till Diwali and during the rest of the period, he worships at Joshimath after which the doors of Badrinath are closed.

Acharya and his disciples are emotionally moved to behold Shri Badrinath temple built at the delightful confluence of the Rivers Rishiganga and Alaknanda. In front can be enjoyed the beauty of the majestic snow-covered peaks of Neelkanth mountains.

The decoration of Badrinath temple satisfies Acharya and he is glad to find the worship of the deity being done according to the scriptures. He gets immersed in devotion of God, sitting like a statue of Lord Vishnu. His poetic sensibilities are awakened and begin to flow in the form of a beautiful poem from his throat. Everyone who is present gets blessed to hear his poem. The poem is in praise of Lord Hari who will now be known as Hari Bhide. However it is the magic of Acharya's voice which gives heavenly joy to the ears of the devotees. The environment appears festive in the presence of Acharya.

Pilgrims from all over the country, after bathing in the strong and extremely cool waves of Alaknanda, desire to meet Acharya before proceeding to the temple and seeing Lord Badri Vishal.

Acharya's teachings continue among the pupils, but the disciples feel that as their *guru* is becoming more self-oriented, his energy is getting attached to the outside world and moving towards his own inner self.

Acharya stands in meditative silence after reciting his sparkling poetry in front of Lord Badrinarayan. The visitors raise slogans in his praise and that of Lord Badrinarayan.

After a few moments, the Acharya returns to earth and descends from the steps of the temple after bowing his head. The crowd jostles with each other to catch a glimpse of the monk and touch his feet. Surrounded by his able-bodied disciples, he blesses all with his loving eyes. Both his hands are raised in the gesture of blessings and the devotees feel gratified at his benevolence.

□

67

Kedarnath

After a few days of stay and sermonising on the banks of Alaknanda in Badrinath, Acharya wishes to visit Kedarnath, but seeing his weak physical condition, the disciples are not willing. They request him to rest in Joshimath, but Acharya's determination is firm.

After staying for two days at Joshimath, he returns to Rudraprayag to spend a night there. Next morning he leaves Rudraprayag to go to Gauri Kund. He is extremely satisfied to see idols of Goddess Gauri and other deities duly worshipped at Gauri Kund.

At the request of local devotees and disciples, he holds a spiritual discourse at Gauri Kund for two days. On the third day, in the wee hours, the team starts ascending towards Kedarnath. Each is reminded of his experience on the Kailash Mansarovar *yatra.* It is a very difficult climb and with the rising afternoon sun, the pilgrims cross Araam Chatti, Jangal Chatti and reach Rambada to stay overneight. The disciples perspire after undertaking this difficult climb under the scorching sun.

Everyone drinks fresh and cold water in Rambada, dry their perspiration and moved. While walking, they reach Garuda Chatti and the golden urn of the temple becomes visible as soon as they cross Garuda Chatti. Everyone bows his head in reverence and looks forward to going inside. The temple spire seems to get bigger on drawing closer with each step. Behind the temple spire can be seen faintly the icy peaks of the mountains underneath the clouds.

After reaching the temple, everyone pays a devotional visit to the *jyotirlinga*. The four rivers – Milky Ganga, Ardhganga, Swarna Dulari and Saraswati flow down from the backdrop of glittering Kedar mountains and merge into River Mandakini. Acharya goes behind the Kedarnath temple to see the beautiful icy Kedar mountain peak and comes to a decision after pondering for a while. On reaching the resting place with the disciples, he goes into solitude. After retiring from the evening worship, he calls all the disciples with a glowing face which has an unusual aura around it. His eyes are full of the same self-confidence that makes him a winner every time.

With love and compassion, his voice echoes, "My dear souls, my life journey is nearing completion and your worship of the *guru* has been unwavering in its devotion. You all have saved India's religion and culture from being destroyed. The crisis to our way of life caused by the catastrophic waves of religious differences, mutual bitterness, vested interests, pretence, hypocrisy, rebellion has been averted with unity, dialogue, equality and fraternity, but, my children, your duty would be more difficult after I leave. The times to come will be indebted to you for saving an ancient culture from getting destroyed.

"India is not just a nation; it is a playground of humanity. This holy land should always remain strong and alert. This is the duty of each one of us who guards the nation in every era. You may forget everything – your identity or even me, but do not forget your duty.

"It's time for my departure. If you have any doubts, then feel free to ask."

On hearing these words of the Acharya, a wave of sorrow spreads among the disciples. The fear due to which they had been disturbed for the past several days, now stares at them with certainty. They were all monks whom the world considered to be devoid of any desires because they had left their home, parents, brothers, friends, happiness and wealth and never looked back since then. Now their *guru* was their parent, brother, assistant, ruler, friend and the prime basis of their life. Not only their daily routine and worship at night, but every moment of their life was dependent on their *guru*.

The *guru* was dear to them as much as life. He used to ask about their diet before taking alms, pacify their curiosity and answer spiritual and worldly questions. When troubled, he used to show them the way. What would now be their future without such an affectionate *guru*? The distraught disciples are unable to control their tears waiting to pour down. Even their wisdom cannot stop their tears.

Guruji too is trying to keep his emotions under control. He says, "I give you my blessings that your wishes are always fulfilled and may you always be revered in the form of Brahma.' Having said this and blessing his disciples, *guruji* gets up and enters his secluded room.

The next day is the day of *Baisakh Purnima*. Acharya gets up in the wee hours, visits Kedarnath after taking a bath and remains immersed in meditation. From here, he returns to the temple and asks his disciples to remain there. Wiping the torrent of tears, the disciples stand there, blinded by the dignity of the *guru's* command. Acharya walks away on the path taken by the Pandavas to heaven in the freezing snows of Mount Kedar. He keeps on walking, going so far till he becomes a hazy figure, faintly visible. This vision gradually becomes more and more blurried before disappearing. The non-dual becomes a reality and the radiant body now becomes snow in the snow. It is difficult to say if light had merged with the supreme effulgence like a crest.

Hundreds and thousands of miles from here, it is the time for evening prayers in the temples of Somnath, Omkareshwar, Rameshwaram, Kashi Vishwanath where ubiquitous devotees seek blessings in the holy aura of *jyotirlingas.* Yes, even at Dharmarajeshwar in Malwa, old priests are engaged in worshipping Shiva and Vishnu with enthusiasm, while the bitter struggle between the Shaivas and Vaishnavas is now confined to memory.

□□□